BUYING A HOME

WHEN YOU'RE SINGLE

BUYING A HOME
WHEN YOU'RE SINGLE

Donna G. Albrecht

JOHN WILEY & SONS, INC.

New York • Chichester • Brisbane • Toronto • Singapore

This text is printed on acid-free paper.

Library of Congress Cataloging-in-Publication Data:

Albrecht, Donna G.
        Buying a home when you're single / by Donna
    Albrecht.
            p.   cm.
        Includes index.
        ISBN 0-471-02499-6 (acid-free paper)

Printed in the United States of America.

10   9   8   7

This book is dedicated to my husband, Mike, and our daughter, Abby, for their incredible support and patience through the research and writing of this project.

Acknowledgments

One thing my many years of writing about real estate for consumers has given me is a deep respect for the generosity of many experts and organizations in the real estate industry.

Many have freely shared their expertise with me (and through this book, you). Because of their generosity, I am able to give you the best, up-to-date information available. I would especially like to express my gratitude to the National Association of Realtors, National Council of State Housing Agencies, National Association of the Remodeling Industry, American Land Title Association, California Land Title Association, Community Associations Institute, National Association of Mortgage Brokers, Mortgage Bankers Association of America, American Society of Home Inspectors, *Remodeling Magazine,* and New Orleans' Neighborhood Development Foundation.

I owe a debt of gratitude to some skilled professionals who were instrumental by providing their professional expertise, including Douglas L. Pitchford, Michael D. Barry, Sereta Churchill, and Greg Warner.

Finally, my thanks to all the single home buyers who talked with me about their special concerns and needs. Many of their stories (although some have fictionalized names) are included in this book to illustrate different points being made.

Contents

Contents

Contents

Introduction

If you are still waiting for Prince or Princess Charming to gallop up on a white horse before you buy a home of your own, wake up! It's time to take control of your life.

Now, imagine yourself owning your own home. Someplace where *you,* not a landlord, have control.

Whether you eagerly look forward to abandoning stark white painted walls for soothing colors or hunger for the opportunity to design your kitchen to meet your culinary skills, you are reading this book because you believe you are ready to take control of the environment you live in. And you can.

Whether you are never married, divorced, or widowed, you are a part of the fastest growing segment of the home buying public.

According to figures from the National Association of Realtors, 37 percent of first-time buyers in 1988–89 (the latest figures available) were single males or females with or without dependents and unmarried couples. This was a rise from 29 percent in 1986–87. Even including repeat buyers (which tends to include more families moving up to bigger homes), singles still bought over one-quarter of the homes sold during that period!

Farewell To Fear

Yet, too often, fear keeps singles from getting the home they want and deserve. Nancy Godfrey knows that fear. She wanted the security of owning her own home, but the worry that she might have problems making her payments (even though she has a secure job as travel manager for a major oil company) was overwhelming.

The idea of buying a condo was an enormous commitment for Godfrey. Since childhood, she had internalized societal messages telling her that women do not deserve a home of their own unless they are married and that good people do not have financial debts. She candidly admits that not having a partner to lean on if a problem occurs was a constant factor in her considerations.

At the same time, she realized that she was not living the lifestyle she really wanted. Godfrey loves diversity. One of her great joys is living in San Francisco where diversity is not only tolerated, it is celebrated.

However, she was renting in the desirable Marina neighborhood and finding that the diversity she loved was not evident there. Worse, home prices were escalating at a frightening pace and it looked as if she did not take a chance and buy now, she might be priced out of the market forever.

Summoning her courage, Godfrey stepped out of her safe habitat, paid off her credit cards to reduce the stress caused by debt, and found a homey condominium in the ethnically and socially diverse Haight/Ashbury neighborhood.

Now happily settled in her condo, Godfrey advises others that if something is keeping them too scared to buy a home—whether that something is social, attitudinal, or financial—they should tackle it head on. "There is something very wonderful about being in your own home," Godfrey says contentedly.

Magnets For Singles

San Francisco is one of several major metropolitan areas that tend to attract singles who are likely to buy homes of their own. Chicago and Ft. Lauderdale are other places that are most likely to have singles who buy. San Francisco also has the distinction of having the highest proportion of unmarried couples purchasing homes.

However, strong sales to singles were recorded throughout the country including: 29 percent of the buyers in Chicago, 32 percent in Ft. Lauderdale, 26 percent each in Pittsburgh and Phoenix, 32 percent in Seattle, and a whopping 42 percent in San Francisco.

A Taxing Subject

Buying a home has probably become even more attractive to you every April when you fill out your income tax forms and realize that your stack of rent receipts is not good for much of anything except as fuel for starting a fire. Depending on your tax bracket, you could expect to save at least 28 percent of your mortgage interest payment and real estate taxes if you had made those same payments on a home of your own.

Taxes become a special concern if you have recently come out of a marriage with half the equity in your previously jointly-owned home. Your tax advisor may tell you that you need to reinvest that money in a new home within a certain time frame or risk giving a lot of it to Uncle Sam in capital gains taxes.

As you read *Buying A Home When You're Single,* you will be taken step-by-step through the home buying process and taught the terms and techniques that can be a little intimidating to people who have not faced them before. The experience should also demonstrate opportunities you may not have been aware of before.

If you have thought you could not buy a home because your income or savings did not seem large enough, pay special attention to the techniques and programs that help people with low/moderate income and/or virtually no savings get a home of their own. These programs are successful and they could be your ticket to home ownership.

One caution: laws, regulations, and common practices in an industry like real estate can and do change from time to time (and even from place to place) and may be interpreted in different ways. Because of this diversity, please use this book as a resource—but not a final authority—and consult professionals with your personal questions involving the fine points of local law or real estate practice.

Now, it's time to make your dreams come true. Turn the page—and go for it!

1

A Home Isn't Always A House

Evaluate Your Personal Priorities

When you think of buying a home, what do you visualize? A traditional home on a tree-shaded lane? A condominium high above the street noises with a balcony overlooking twinkling city lights? Maybe you want a townhouse in a planned neighborhood with lots of built-in recreation.

When you buy a home, you are buying more than shelter. You are also buying a lifestyle. Like the clothes you wear and the car you drive, your home will say a lot about how you see yourself and at the same time, it will define some of the opportunities available to you. For instance, kinds of recreation, shopping, and social life you will enjoy there.

There are also trade-offs to consider. If you work in an urban area, maybe you have felt you could only afford a small condo or co-op but you want to live in a more suburban atmosphere. Here, the trade-off might be considering a longer commute to work in order to buy a larger or nicer home.

Buying a Home When You're Single

Change Your Home And Your Lifestyle

In Lexington, Kentucky, Stephen Risner admits that for the first few years after his divorce, buying a home for himself was not a priority. His work and his very active social life kept him as busy as he wanted to be. As manager of computer operations services for Ashland Oil, Inc. he had a comfortable lifestyle. Yet he couldn't quite ignore his friends' persistent advice that he should buy a home.

Along with that, Risner was discovering that he was not meeting the kind of people he was interested in by hanging out in bars. As he made decisions about how to change his lifestyle to something he would get more satisfaction from, he decided to buy a home. Risner chose a small "garden" home with lots of windows looking out to beautiful views. One part of the rental scene he had enjoyed was the amenities, so he was careful to buy a home that came with a pool and tennis courts for residents of the development.

While he admits that the social life in the development has not been quite what he expected, he is enjoying it nonetheless and he loves his home. Most of the residents are families and the community activities are designed for them, so other singles tend to stay away. If he were to do it again today, Risner thinks he would have asked his agent more questions about the single lifestyle at this development. However, he notes that the excellent location of his home does make it a very good investment, which was one point he had stressed with his agent.

There has been one unexpected benefit that he talks of happily. After many years of living apart from him, his son and daughter have both moved in while they go to college and he is really enjoying this time with them.

What Do You Want?

Before you rush out to look at open-houses this weekend, first determine exactly what it is you want in a home.

Some features will be determined by your preferred lifestyle. If you entertain a lot, you may want a dining room, a big kitchen and/or a spacious, sunny patio. If you work at home, a comfortable office is a must. If your St. Bernard loves to dig, you need a yard.

6

On the other hand, some features you choose will be determined by your personal vision of your private life. Do you like to wake up with the sun streaming in your window? Do you want a home with a bay window for your Christmas tree? Do high ceilings make your spirit soar? These can all reflect emotional choices that have a real place in your home buying decision because choosing a home with the features that are important to you can be the difference between living in a place and really being at home.

Location, Location, Location

Whenever anyone asks what are the three most important things to remember when buying real estate, the answer is always, "Location, location, location." Location is one of the first things you need to consider when you are beginning to look for a home to buy. Use these questions to help you focus in on the kind of location that best suits you.

* How far are you willing to commute? If 30 minutes each way is your absolute maximum, then take a map and draw a perimeter showing the total area you are willing to look in—and save yourself a lot of time by staying within those borders.

Since commuting longer each day than you are comfortable with will become a constant source of irritation, it can affect how much you enjoy your home. You may prefer to have two area perimeters. The first is for your preferred commute time, and the other is for the time and distance you will be willing to settle for in exchange for other desirable features.

* Do you want to live near other singles? If you do, you will want to talk to others about neighborhoods that attract more singles. Obvious choices could be areas that are near colleges or universities, multi-unit developments that specialize in studio or one-bedroom units, or even neighborhoods that attract people with similar lifestyle choices like the Castro in San Francisco.

If you are not already familiar with the communities you are considering buying in, talk with several sources about the character of different developments or neighborhoods. Obvious places to start would be with real estate agents. Surprisingly, even if you are not being transferred, relocation specialists (which many real estate offices have) are often willing to counsel you free in hopes you will later choose an agent from their office.

Another place to find other singles who may be able to give you insight would be the library. If you are not familiar with the area, the librarian can refer you to organizations you may already be part of, like Parents Without Partners, or tell you about active local groups you might never have heard of. The contact names you get from the librarian are likely to be people who know a lot of other singles and can give you some ideas about neighborhoods where you are likely to find an active singles network.

* What are your shopping habits? Do you love to be able to walk out your front door and do your everyday shopping within a few blocks? Do you think nothing of hopping in the car and driving 10 minutes to get a loaf of bread?

If you are the first, you will probably enjoy living in an established neighborhood or a small town. Some newer communities are being built to what architects call "pedestrian scale," which simply means that they are designed to allow residents to handle many of their everyday needs without using a car.

If jumping into the car is comfortable for you, you may want to look at suburban neighborhoods. If you are thinking about a rural lifestyle, you will need to accept the time it will take you to get to and from shopping and other activities.

* Do you want to be near schools? There can be several good reasons for living within walking distance of schools. The obvious reason is because you have (or expect to have) children who will use them. If you have no children, then investment may be a factor influencing your choice.

Traditionally, homes near to good quality schools appreciate more quickly than similar homes that are not close to schools. The trick here is to check with real estate agents and the school district to see if the school is one that has good ratings and is attractive to incoming families. On the other hand, the good investment of a home near a school can become less desirable if having a lot of children living nearby bothers you.

* **Are you active in community activities?** Is it important to you to spend time involved in church, cultural or social activities? Then you will want to live in an area where these activities are available nearby.

* **What other amenities do you want near your new home?** Think for a few minutes about what community amenities you count on and want to be near. Do you want to be close to a good library? Is nearby medical care important? Would you like to be able to take public transportation to work? If you travel a lot, how far are you comfortable traveling just to get to the airport?

* **Where do you feel safe and how important is it to you?** Safety is a basic human need, but everyone has a different comfort level. For some, the excitement and energy urban neighborhoods provide more than balance off any nervousness about safety. For others, that same neighborhood may be a constant source of fear. There are no right or wrong answers. Your own experiences will determine what kind of environment you need to feel safe.

Working It Out On Paper

By now, you should have a pretty good idea of the environment you want for your new home. Enter your decisions on the worksheet on pages 15-16. If you are considering buying a home with another single, each of you should separately study the questions above and fill out separate worksheets. Then arrange a time when you can get together to compare your answers.

If you each have similar visions of the lifestyle you plan to lead, great! If not, you may want to spend more time talking to each other about how you want to live before you go any further. You may even want to work with a counselor or real estate agent who can help you reach an acceptable compromise. But if you can not come to an agreement, you may want to reconsider whether you should buy with this particular person.

Styles Of Housing

There are many different kinds of housing you can choose from. Along with the traditional single-family detached house, there are

9

duets (sometimes called duplexes or half-doubles), townhouses, condominiums, cooperatives, and even factory-constructed homes (including mobile homes, modular homes, kit homes, and log homes). Each has its own advantages and disadvantages. Some also come with homeowners associations which have their own benefits and problems (see Chapter 2).

SINGLE-FAMILY DETACHED— This traditional home stands alone on a lot. On the plus side, you have a great deal of privacy and more control over your property than you are likely to have with the other forms. Unless there are homeowners association restrictions, you can paint the house whatever color you like, add on rooms, knock down walls, and landscape to your personal tastes—the only power you answer to is your community's building permit department.

With no walls connecting your home to others, you are less likely to be bothered by your neighbor's activities. At the same time, you will be responsible for all the maintenance and upkeep, inside and out, and when major repairs like roof replacement have to be done, they are all yours too.

CONDOMINIUM— As a condominium owner, you will be buying your unit (as it is defined in the Condominium Plan for your development) as well as a proportional interest in all the common areas in the development. While the term "condominium" often is thought to refer to an apartment-like attached home, that is not necessarily true.

Condominium is technically a type of interest in land involving specific characteristics including: common ownership of the property; required membership in an association which controls the use of the commonly owned property; and adherence to the condominium's Covenants, Conditions and Restrictions (CC&R's).

A condominium development will normally include common areas ranging from walkways and utility rooms to pools. Luxurious condominiums may also have common areas for golf courses, equestrian trails, and clubhouses. All exterior maintenance is handled by the homeowners association.

10

You will be responsible to pay assessments to finance the maintenance of the common areas, and there will be CC&R's which may be written in a way that put some restrictions on how you can use your home and have some impact on your lifestyle (see Chapter 2).

TOWNHOUSE— While you may think of a townhouse as an attached home of two or more stories, this form of ownership is more a description of a housing style than a legal description of a type of ownership interest in land. Your townhouse may legally be a condominium, a unit or lot in a Planned Unit Development, or a single-family detached home.

DUETS— In some areas, this style of housing is called a duplex or half-double. It is a construction of one building which incorporates two homes. Both units may be owned by the same person, or they may be sold separately.

CO-OPS— A cooperative has a corporation which owns the entire project. The home units and all common facilities are included as a single property and as the homeowner you will own stock in the corporation. You receive the right to occupy a unit in the cooperative because you are a shareholder. One other factor that sets co-ops apart from condominiums is that the managing board of the co-op has the ability to control who buys each unit and can accept or reject you, as a buyer, for any reason.

FACTORY-CONSTRUCTED HOMES— According to Tony Hadley, spokesperson for the California Manufactured Housing Institute, "factory-constructed homes" is a phrase used to cover the spectrum of homes which are pre-built in factories rather than stick-built on-site. These homes are often more affordable than traditional stick-built homes in the same community. In addition, they may be built in park-like communities or right on a single-family lot. Below are some descriptions of three common types of factory-constructed homes.

MANUFACTURED HOME— a factory-built home that meets the National Manufactured Home Construction & Safety Standards set by HUD.

MODULAR HOME— a factory-built home that meets state and/or local building codes, but not necessarily the HUD regulations.

MOBILE HOMES— a type of factory-constructed home that is built to voluntary industry standards— not a particular set of governmental regulations. This term is often a misnomer. The homes are rarely mobile once they are put on site. They are also often clustered in parks that can offer social activities and a feeling of community while providing the degree of privacy often associated with single-family detached homes.

Just What She Wanted

Affordability was definitely a factor for Pauline Goodin when she purchased her mobile home in Lakeland, Florida, but finances weren't the only consideration. Personal security was also a major concern because now that her children were raised, she would be living in her new home alone. For Goodin, the answer was to choose a mobile home in a park that had a special security patrol to watch out for the safety of the residents.

Is Buying Really For You?

This may seem like a strange question to ask in a book about buying a home. But it is something you should ask yourself before signing on the dotted line. Your marital status has much less to do with your readiness to buy a home than your lifestyle does. A performer who always has to be ready to move where the work is, is much less likely to be ready to buy a home than a teacher or police officer who expects to stay in one community for many years. Your local economy will also have some influence on whether you should buy right now.

Are Homes In Your Area A Good Investment?

While there are income tax benefits for home ownership, there can be financial reasons why buying a home, right here and right now, may be a mistake.

When the economy of a community depends on one major industry which is having problems, there may be a lot of attractively priced homes available. Unfortunately, until the area's economy is revitalized, it may be all but impossible to sell your home again at any price. If you know you will live in the area for a long time, these distressed properties may make excellent long-term investments.

If you think you might move on, it may be better to rent. Renting can be especially economical since distressed sellers may be willing to rent to you at very attractive rates. If you are considering buying for investment purposes, you might still be able to achieve your financial goals by pursuing other investments with the income you would have spent on closing fees and higher monthly mortgage payments.

How Will It Affect Your Career Plans?

If you expect to move soon, then buying a home may have fewer or no financial advantages. (Of course, if your employer will pick up some of your selling expenses, it will be more likely to pay.)

Depending on how quickly your house payments lower your mortgage balance and how quickly homes in your area are appreciating, you can normally expect it to take a few years to recoup the transaction expenses you incur when you buy and sell a home.

If you are questioning the purchase, you may want to talk with an accountant who can help you work out the numbers. Be sure your calculations also include consideration for any income tax advantages you will have received during your anticipated ownership.

Do You Really Want To Own A Home?

Don't buy just because all your friends are doing it or your family is pressuring you to settle down. If you are at a stage in your life where the freedom to pick up and move on short notice is important to you, or you just do not have the time or energy to take on more responsibility, renting may be a better choice for now.

Looking back on her experience, Rachel Pollock of Denver realized that buying a home was not the best choice she could have made three years ago. On one hand, she was still mourning her mother's recent death (and the loss of "home" that represented). On the other hand, she was moving to Colorado to be near her young grandchildren who were encouraging her to have a place where they could come and visit.

Then Pollock saw THE HOUSE. Actually, it was more like THE STUDY. She fell in love with a room that had beautiful built-in shelves and stained glass windows in the doors. She conveniently ignored the fact that this large home had four bedrooms and a yard that would require constant care. And she would be living there alone except for the occasional overnight visits by her grandchildren.

The problems started almost immediately. First were the caretaking responsibilities. She did not like dealing with growing grass and toilets that did not flush. A hail storm damaged her roof—when she was out of town on business—forcing her to deal with insurance adjusters long-distance.

Pollock also had violated the first rule of living in the suburbs. She depended on public transportation. Having grown up in New York City and lived in Boston, she was comfortable depending on public transportation to get her where she wanted to go, but her family did not share her feelings. Sometimes, a grandchild would even duck out of the dining room during visits and look in the garage, hoping to find a new car.

Then there was the quiet.

Pollock loves the energy that comes from living in an active, urban area. So when she would go for a walk at night on the dark, quiet streets of her neighborhood, it just felt wrong.

Finally, she realized that the house owned her, not vice versa. So she sold the home and now blissfully lives in a rental situation. She admits that it might have worked out better if she had chosen a condo or townhouse where certain maintenance chores would have been taken care of for her. But she says, that on the balance, she is happier not owning a property at this point in her life.

Lifestyle Choices Worksheet

Before you can find a home you will love, you need to know what you really want. That sounds simple, but if you have not thought things through, it can be easy to be swayed by an attractive feature at one home and ignore the drawbacks until you are actually living with them.

Lifestyle Choices Worksheet

General Lifestyle

CHOICE	NEED	WANT	OPTIONAL	DISLIKE
Climate				
Short Commute				
Near Other Singles				
Good Investment Value				
Privacy				
Safety/Security				
Recreation 　　Tennis 　　Golf 　　Swimming 　　Hiking 　　Parks 　　_____ 　　_____				
T.V./Radio Reception				
Near Public Transportation				
Near Airport				
Near Church/Synagogue				
Good Schools				
Medical Care				
Library				
Shopping (everyday)				
Shopping (major)				
Views				
Parking				
Homeowners Association				

Lifestyle Choices Worksheet

Home Features

CHOICE	NEED	WANT	OPTIONAL	DISLIKE
Luxury Kitchen				
Dining Room				
Patio/Balcony				
Fenced Yard				
Mature Landscaping				
Master Suite				
Office/Study				
Fireplace				
Pool/Spa (or space for one)				
Low Maintenance				
Energy Efficiency				
Air Conditioning				
Dramatic Ceilings High Beamed Cathedral				
Extra Bathroom(s)				
Indoor Laundry				
Adequate Storage				
Space for Pets				
Good Natural Light				
Personal Desires (i.e., bay windows) _____ _____ _____ _____				

2

Association By Gilt

What Is A Homeowners Association?

Homeowners associations. While they may be the last thing on your mind when you are looking for a home, they should be the first thing you ask about. Depending on your personality and the personality of the homeowners association you will be dealing with, you could be dealing with a godsend or a nightmare.

As you make your decision, you will not be alone. According to the Community Associations Institute, the number of homeowners associations has tripled in the last 10 years from 45,000 to about 150,000. Right now, about 35 million Americans live in neighborhoods which are governed by homeowners associations.

The key to a development having a homeowners association is often the common ownership of some property. Whether it is a few square feet at the entrance of the subdivision or extensive open space including amenities like tennis courts and pools, homeowners associations are set up (usually by the builder) to provide a mechanism for the continuing maintenance of those areas.

For some people, the rules and regulations imposed by these associations can be so unattractive that they choose a home in a neighborhood that is free of associations. What those buyers end up possibly lacking in amenities, may be more than balanced in their estimation by the lack of restrictions on how they can use their property. This is a primary consideration you need to make when you are considering the environment you want for your home.

A Rose By Any Other Name

A homeowners association may be known by a variety of names including a property-owners association, cooperative, condominium council, or council of co-owners. The major responsibility of this association is to protect the property owners' investment and enhance and maintain the property owned in common by the members. The association provides for the physical maintenance and operation of all the common facilities including parking areas, private streets, swimming pool(s), landscaped grounds, tennis court(s), and other landscape and recreational amenities.

At the same time, the association can provide defined services for what you may think of as your property such as maintenance of the roof and exterior walls in some developments.

Depending on the individual association, it could have the responsibility of providing for common services which might include security, trash and garbage collection, and snow removal.

Also, while it may only happen occasionally, your association might choose to get involved with local government on issues affecting the neighborhood. For instance, if the city is considering changes to the area roads that could cause new traffic patterns that will affect the neighborhood, the association may want to make sure city planners and/or the city council are aware of their concerns.

What's In It For You?

A primary reason cited for choosing a home in a community that has a homeowners association is that the property values will be maintained. Usually this is the case. As a buyer, you will expect to see a neighborhood that is well maintained and attractive.

The Covenants, Conditions and Restrictions (CC&R's) which govern the neighborhood will usually spell out many of the owner's responsibilities including possibly the timetable for front yard landscaping (if it is the owner's responsibility in that particular development), the colors the home can be painted, and whether owners can add certain amenities, like basketball hoops, to the front of their property.

The CC&R's also can define the situations where a homeowner is allowed to change the look of the front of the house, whether the owner can add rooms, and if TV satellite dishes or ham radio antennae are permissible. For many people, this supplies a comfort level that allows them to relax because the homeowner next door can not paint the place bright purple and park an RV in the driveway in perpetuity.

However, if you find yourself railing against the idea of all the restrictions even before you sign on the dotted line, you may want to look for a different neighborhood.

The benefits of owning a home covered by a homeowners association are especially attractive to singles who are interested in a low-maintenance lifestyle and/or having certain recreational amenities like pools, tennis courts, walking trails, etc., that they might not be able to afford or maintain on their own. Instead of spending your free time pulling weeds, you can lock your door and travel for a few days or weeks without having your home look unkempt.

On The Other Hand

However, if you have always dreamed of painting your house apple green, you could be upset to find that only certain earth tones are permitted in the neighborhood you are interested in. Your dog may be larger than the CC&R's allow, and your plans to make the garage a workshop and park your car on the street may not be possible.

Each homeowners association's CC&R's contain restrictions which might not mesh with your lifestyle. In your opinion, some of them may be negotiable, but the key is to negotiate them before you buy the property.

If you are really excited by a particular home and want to make an offer on it, consider including a contingency clause to cover your particular concern in your offer to buy. The contingency would stipulate that if the homeowners association does not give you a waiver enabling you to pursue your business or permit you to engage in certain activities that are important to you but may be restricted by the CC&R's, you can get out of the contract.

For instance, if you are (or plan to be) running a business from your home, you need to read the CC&R's especially carefully. There may be restrictions on obvious business-related activities like posting a sign in front of your home or having big trucks make deliveries. In some cases, the restrictions may prohibit having any business at all in your home. If you are seriously considering having a home-based business, you should consult your city and county zoning authorities, whether you live in a neighborhood with a homeowners association or not.

If you are planning to occasionally bring home work from the office and do it in your home, you probably do not have a problem. If you are planning a business which requires a business license—you very well might have a problem.

Sometimes the deciding factor in what business activity is permitted is whether the neighbors will be able to see, hear or smell it. So a childcare business that creates traffic and noise may not be acceptable. You may also never be able to get approval to repair cars in your driveway or park the truck you use for business in front of your home. (You may not be able to do this even though you do not have a home-based business. There might be restrictions against bringing home your employer's vehicle.)

At the same time, a consulting business that does not bring clients to the premises or alert the neighbors to its presence in any significant way could be fine. Again, if there is any question, clear it up—in writing—before you complete the purchase.

Avoiding The Dog House

Perhaps the one area that causes more dissension about the benefits of homeowners associations than any others is their restrictions on pets. While each association might have its own individual restrictions, some common ones are controls on the species, number, and size of your pets. Your cocker spaniel may be no problem, but your Labrador retriever may just be too big.

If you are a fan of ferrets or pot-bellied pigs, your pet may not be welcomed by some homeowners associations. There may be leash laws for your dog and/or cat, and you may be required to clean up after your pet if it defecates on association property.

In all fairness, any community (whether it has a homeowners association or not) may have civic regulations about the number of pets you can have, leash laws, and "pooper-scooper" ordinances. So if your pet is an important part of your life, you need to plan ahead.

You should also be aware that homes in some communities without a homeowners association have civic or zoning regulations that can affect your liberties. So if you are looking for a home where you can park your company vehicle out front, put a business sign in front of your home, or set up a ham radio set, you should absolutely check with the civic governing body about the potential restrictions on the activities that interest you.

Sometimes you might feel you are getting away with ignoring the regulations, but sooner or later you may be forced to comply.

If you let your pet run loose, you face the potential of having your special friend picked up by animal control, attacked by other animals, or hit by a car. Your homeowners association may also notify you about your non-compliance with CC&R's restrictions on pets, and the association may pursue legal remedies against you. If you want to be a responsible pet owner and you live in an urban or suburban community, you will be doing your pet a favor by keeping it on a leash whenever you are out of your home or yard, whether it is required by CC&R's, law, or not at all.

"Stretch"ing The Limits

When Peter Mertz bought his condominium in Bethesda, Maryland, he admits that he was more interested in the good deal he was getting than reading the CC&R's (including the leash requirement for dogs—and cats). His cats, Desdemona, Mayberry, and Beau, roamed free and even became favorite visitors to owners at some other units in the development.

Then, on a trip to Atlanta, he rescued a street cat, named her Stretch, and brought her home to join the family. Only Stretch had one little problem. She had a natural affinity for people who were allergic to cats. When a woman with a serious cat allergy moved into a nearby unit, Stretch started waiting outside her door every morning. When she came out for her newspaper, Stretch would bolt inside and hide under her bed.

This woman apparently *had* read the CC&R's. Mertz received a letter from the homeowners association. Then came a visit from a board member who, while explaining the need for Mertz to abide by the CC&R's, mentioned that he would miss mornings on the patio, drinking his coffee with one of Mertz's cats on his lap. Reluctantly, Mertz kept his cats inside until he was able to move to a house with a big yard where the cats roam outside today.

Dollars And Sense

The Price Is (Or May Be) Right

Nothing in life is free—especially membership in a homeowners association. Except in very rare cases, buying a home in a development with a homeowners association obligates you to pay the assessments charged by that association. Since it is your money, you need to look at the association very carefully before signing on the dotted line.

The assessment may be payable monthly, quarterly or annually. It can be based on a per-unit charge or vary according to the size or value of the unit. If you fail to make the payments, the association may place a lien against your property—in the worst case scenario, your home can be sold to satisfy that debt.

When you are looking at assessments, it can be enticing to go for the lowest payment. However, as in other areas of life, you get what you pay for.

The first thing to look for is what the assessment covers. An assessment that only covers a neighborhood pool can reasonably be expected to be lower than an assessment for a neighborhood featuring a pool, walking trails, and a clubhouse (but be sure to factor in the number of homes supporting each association).

What To Ask

Three questions you need to ask yourself and your real estate agent are:

ARE THE ASSESSMENTS REASONABLE? The assessments can be pegged unreasonably low especially in new developments. The builder may "low ball" the assessment and make up the difference during the sales period to make the development appear more affordable. When the association is turned over to the residents, the assessment will likely have to be raised to meet its responsibilities. It can be a good idea to compare the assessments for the neighborhood you are interested in with assessments for other developments with similar amenities.

IS THERE AN ADEQUATE "SINKING FUND"? The budget should include arrangements for building cash reserves for major maintenance and replacements. Even if your development is new, it will require expensive repairs and maintenance sooner and later. If there are no reserves established to pay for these expenses and they occur anyway, you may face a special assessment to cover the expenses. Again, paying these assessments is not voluntary—it is compulsory—even if the timing is not convenient for you.

ARE THE ASSESSMENTS RESPONSIVE TO CHANGING NEEDS? Your association's expenses can increase over time. Common causes include tax increases, wage increases for employees, and higher management costs. If your association is tied to a set fee or a specific rate of assessment increase, it may not be able to keep up with increases in real costs for the taxes, maintenance, and services the association requires. That could mean sacrificing necessary services if expenses for those services exceed the amount available to sustain them. To ensure the health of the association and its ability to meet its responsibilities, it is important that the assessment can be increased a reasonable amount whenever necessary.

When you are considering buying a home included in a homeowners association, your real estate agent should supply you with all pertinent documents about the development, including the CC&R's and financial documents about the association.

You may want to have an attorney or CPA who works regularly with homeowners associations look over the documents and give you an opinion about the health of the organization and potential downstream problems that you could face if you buy this property. To avoid any possible conflict of interest, choose an attorney or CPA who does not have professional ties to the association you are checking out. Again, if you are making an offer before you receive these documents, you may want to include a contingency clause in your offer stating that your completion of the contract is conditional on your receiving a positive opinion from your attorney and/or accountant.

In addition, it is important to ask if there are any lawsuits pending or contemplated against the builder for problems like defective construction or against the homeowners association by other owners.

Getting The Most For Your Money

The best way to protect your investment is to be active in your homeowners association. Much like the government of a small community, the association controls how your neighborhood or building looks and the kind and quality of services you can expect.

The association has the responsibility to enforce the master regulations and architectural controls, and plan social and recreational activities. From time to time, the board will have to make decisions about matters affecting your lifestyle. If you attend meetings and possibly serve on the board or affiliated committees, you will have a voice in making the decisions.

3

How Much Home Can You Afford?

Why You Should Prequalify For A Loan

If you have done it, you know. It really hurts to fall in love with a home only to find out that you can't possibly afford to buy it. Fortunately, you can avoid this problem by prequalifying for a mortgage.

Most lenders are eager to help you through this process in hopes that when you are ready to take out a mortgage, you will come back to them—although you are not committed to doing so.

In fact, prequalifying is not a commitment process. You disclose your assets, income, expenses, and liabilities and the lender tells you (and often gives you a letter stating) how much of a mortgage you are likely to qualify for. This letter is not the same thing as a loan commitment. It states the maximum loan value, maximum interest rate, maximum loan-to-value of the property, and type of loan (Fixed-Rate, Adjustable-Rate, FHA, VA, etc.) for which you appear to qualify.

Prequalifying has two strong advantages for you as a buyer. First, you will save time and emotional wear and tear by limiting your home search to properties you may be able to buy. Happily, like many others, you may be pleasantly surprised to find you can qualify for a larger mortgage than you originally imagined.

Second, if you are buying during a seller's market, the seller of a home you are making an offer on may be more inclined to accept your offer than one made by someone whose ability to qualify for a mortgage is in question.

In fact, in meeting with a lender to prequalify, you are giving yourself an opportunity for a no-stress exploration of your options. As a single, your household income may be less than your married friends with dual incomes. But that does not necessarily mean you can only afford half as much house. During your prequalification process, you and your lender can explore your individual financial situation, and your lender should be able to point out the pros and cons of different financing options as they apply to you. He or she will also be able to point out special first-time and/or income related home buyer programs which are available.

This is the time to ask about any ideas you have about improving your ability to borrow. For instance, if you plan to take in room-mates, can you count anticipated rental income on your application? Not likely. However, if you buy a home together with a friend, both your incomes can be used to help you qualify for a mortgage.

Sarah Gallagher, a high school teacher, had become very discouraged because even though she was a skilled professional, her income was not enough to enable her to buy a single-family home in the pricey San Francisco Bay Area where she lived. She had already dismissed the idea of buying a condominium because she wanted more privacy and control over who lived right next to her than she could get in a condo development. She was also certain that she did not want a roommate.

Her real estate agent came up with a twist on the roommate idea that solved her problem: a duplex (or duet). Since one unit is a rental, her lender allowed her to count much of the anticipated rent as income to her—raising the amount of monthly income she had available. This in turn helped her qualify for a large enough mortgage to buy. Best of all, she has the privacy she wanted and can choose the tenants who live next to her. (If the property were to be sublet, she might not have as much freedom since the landlord's right to control who sublets a rental may be restricted under some rent control laws.)

How To Prequalify

Once you have chosen a lender (see more on this in Chapter 4) you need to gather some documentation before you meet with her. If you are salaried, you will need:

1. W-2's for the last two years
2. A recent pay statement
3. Savings and checking account statements
4. Documents relating to liquid assets like stocks or mutual funds
5. Stock certificates held privately
6. IRA statements
7. Documents verifying any other assets you plan to liquefy to buy the home (i.e., insurance policies you plan to take the cash value out of, cars you plan to sell)

If you are self-employed, bring in your last two tax returns along with the other documents.

You will also need to bring documentation of outstanding debts and on-going commitments, like charge accounts and car payments, as well as paid-up accounts. The paid-up accounts become especially important if you have paid off some debts in anticipation of buying a home since the creditors may not have reported your paid-up status to the credit bureau yet. On the other hand, you should be aware that all of your *potential* debt can be considered as current debt in your mortgage application. This can include high credit limits on accounts—whether you have ever gone up to those limits or not.

While this is substantially the same information you will have to supply when you eventually submit your loan application, it is much less formal. The lender is not likely to verify the information because this stage is primarily informational. The amount you prequalify for is based on the figures you give.

When you make your formal application, all your data is subject to verification before you get your loan commitment. Normally, if you get a letter from a lender stating that you have prequalified, you will be able to (more or less) get the mortgage described in the letter. On rare occasions, it will not work out. The primary reasons are: (1) the process was somehow faulty (an unfortunately broad category); (2) you held back negative information; (3) your personal financial picture changed (maybe you got laid-off); (4) the lending climate has changed (for instance, interest rates went up); or (5) the property you have chosen does not appraise for the amount needed to justify the loan commitment.

How Much Are You Likely To Qualify For?

Before you meet with a lender, you may want to have some idea of where you are heading. Working out your mortgage potential can give you a rough idea of what you can qualify for. However, remember that working with a lender who can match your personal situation to currently available loans will give you the best overall picture.

As a general rule, your housing expenses should be between 25 percent to 33 percent of your total income (housing expense divided by gross income) for a fixed-rate loan. This is the top figure in what lenders refer to as your ratios. Ratios look like fractions, but the top and bottom numbers are both percentages of your total income. The more of a down payment you make, the higher the figures can be.

The bottom ratio is your total monthly expense (housing plus liabilities) divided by your gross income. For a fixed-rate loan, the bottom ratio should normally be between 28 percent and 38 percent. As you can see, the extra allowance for other liabilities is not large. If you are considering adding to your debt by buying a car, taking an expensive vacation, etc., you will find that waiting until after you buy your home can make it much easier to qualify for your mortgage.

One thing to remember is that these ratios are not set in concrete. Certainly, if your ratios are lower than these examples, you are in very good shape. If your ratios are higher than shown, you may have to work harder with your lender to find an appropriate loan, or you may need to work on paying off your debt before you buy.

Before going to the chart on page 30, figure what 25 percent of your gross monthly income is. Check with local lenders or look at interest rates currently reported and/or advertised in your local news-paper. Go across to the current interest rate and down to 25 percent of your gross income. Follow that horizontal line to the left to get a rough idea of the size mortgage you can expect to qualify for. For a more detailed estimate, use the charts in Appendix II.

When you actually apply for your mortgage, you will find that other expenses like taxes and insurance are included in your housing costs for evaulation purposes. On the other hand, lenders will often let you have housing costs of 1/3 of your gross income or more depending on your personal financial situation and the type of loan you are applying for.

Another chart to help you determine the kind of loan you might qualify for is shown on page 31 (Appendix II contains charts with a broader range of information). If you are buying with a friend, add their income and liability figures besides yours and include them in your total.

Maximum Monthly Payments Chart
(30-year fixed-rate mortgage)

Loan Amount	Interest Rate								
	8%	8.5%	9.0%	9.5%	10.0%	10.5%	11.0%	11.5%	12.0%
$ 20,000	$ 147	$ 154	$ 161	$ 168	$ 175	$ 183	$ 190	$ 198	$ 206
25,000	183	192	201	210	219	229	238	248	257
30,000	220	231	241	252	263	274	286	297	309
35,000	257	269	282	294	307	320	333	347	360
40,000	293	308	322	336	351	366	381	396	411
45,000	330	346	362	378	395	412	429	446	463
50,000	367	384	402	420	439	457	476	495	514
55,000	404	423	443	462	483	503	524	545	566
60,000	440	461	483	505	527	549	571	594	517
65,000	477	500	523	547	570	595	619	644	669
70,000	514	538	563	589	614	640	667	693	720
75,000	550	577	603	631	658	686	714	743	771
80,000	587	615	644	673	702	732	762	792	823
85,000	624	654	684	715	746	778	809	842	874
90,000	660	692	724	757	790	823	857	891	926
95,000	697	730	764	799	834	869	905	941	977
100,000	734	769	805	841	878	915	952	990	1,029
110,000	807	846	885	925	965	1,006	1,048	1,089	1,132
120,000	880	923	966	1,009	1,053	1,098	1,143	1,188	1,234
130,000	954	1,000	1,046	1,093	1,141	1,189	1,238	1,287	1,337
140,000	1,027	1,076	1,126	1,177	1,229	1,281	1,333	1,386	1,440
150,000	1,101	1,153	1,207	1,261	1,316	1,372	1,428	1,485	1,543
160,000	1,174	1,230	1,287	1,345	1,404	1,464	1,524	1,584	1,646
170,000	1,247	1,307	1,368	1,429	1,492	1,555	1,619	1,684	1,749
180,000	1,321	1,384	1,448	1,514	1,580	1,647	1,714	1,783	1,852
190,000	1,394	1,461	1,529	1,598	1,667	1,738	1,809	1,882	1,954
200,000	1,468	1,538	1,609	1,682	1,755	1,829	1,905	1,981	2,057

To use the chart, find the current interest rate and your approximate loan amount and then read across to where they meet, which is your maximum monthly payment. You can use the mortgage work sheet to help you find the maximum monthly payment you can afford. Or, after determining 25 percent of your gross income and dividing by 12 to find the maximum payment you can make on a 90 percent loan with 10 percent down, you can locate that amount on the chart and see the maximum loan you can afford at various interest rates. Remember to factor in the down payment, too. Sources: NATIONAL ASSOCIATION OF REALTORS®; National Association of Home Builders

Qualification Assessment Chart*

INCOME	Amount
Base Earnings	_____
Overtime	_____
Bonuses/Commissions	_____
Dividends & Interest	_____
Other_____	_____
TOTAL	$_____
	(A) Gross Income

HOUSING EXPENSE	CURRENT	PROPOSED
Principal & Interest (use your estimate from the last chart for "Proposed")	_____	_____
2nd Mortgage (if any)	_____	_____
Taxes	_____	_____
Hazard/Fire Insurance	_____	_____
Homeowners Assn. Dues	_____	_____
Other _____	_____	_____
TOTAL	$_____	$_____
		(B) Housing Cost

LIABILITIES OVER 10 MONTHS	AMOUNT
Auto Loan	_____
Credit Union Loan	_____
Student Loan	_____
5% of Total Credit Card Balance	_____
Child Support	_____
Other _____	_____
TOTAL	$_____
	(C) Liabilities

POTENTIAL MONTHLY EXPENSE

_____ + _____ = _____

(B) Housing Cost   (C) Liabilities   (D) Total Monthly Expense

QUALIFYING RATIOS

Top Ratio (B/A): $_____ Divided by $_____ = _____%
Bottom Ratio (D/A): $_____ Divided by $_____ = _____%

* This chart is adapted from one provided by Financial Transaction Corporation, Danville, CA. Used with permission.

Below are some typical ratios. LTV means Loan To Value. If you make a 5% down payment, your LTV is 95%. If your down payment is 20%, your LTV is 80%. As you can see, the more money you put down, the easier it is to qualify in terms of the percentage of your income which can go toward housing and other monthly expenses.

LTV	Fixed-Rate Mortgage		Adjustable-Rate Mortgage	
	Top	Bottom	Top	Bottom
95%	25%	28%	N/A	N/A
90%	28%	36%	30%	36%
80%	33%	38%	33%	38%

A Taxing Subject

Property taxes are an unfortunate fact of life. Depending on where you live, they can be relatively stable, or can go up dramatically when the property is sold (especially in California). Your real estate agent should be able to help you determine the tax burden you will face. Be aware that even if the taxes for the year are paid, you almost always become responsible for paying your *pro rata* share of the annual tax bite at closing.

The Last Word—Closing Costs

Not so long ago, closing costs were often referred to as "hidden costs," since buyers only found out the full extent of them at the closing. Fortunately, the federal government's Real Estate Settlement Procedures Act (RESPA) covers most of the real estate loans you are likely to apply for including VA, FHA, and other loans eligible to be sold on the secondary market.

You should know that while local tradition often determines whether the buyer or seller pays particular expenses, you may be able to lower your costs by careful shopping and/or negotiating.

In the shopping category, you can choose the attorney you hire. In some areas it is customary to hire an attorney to represent you. In other areas, you may decide to hire an attorney, especially for a complicated deal. You can also choose the insurance company you buy your fire and hazard insurance from and the title company you use. The amount of expense you can negotiate down will depend in part on the state of the local real estate market. Sellers in a down market may be more willing to pay some expenses traditionally paid by buyers if that is what it takes to complete the deal.

One expense sometimes falls into an unusual category—paid by the agent. Home warranty policies cover repair or replacement of designated systems and appliances for the length of the policy. While this can be a great benefit to you (especially if the hot water heater springs a leak the day after you move in!), many agents and sellers see these policies as relieving them of potential legal hassles if something goes wrong soon after the sale. Because of this, some agents now routinely pay the cost of these policies—and many others can be talked into it.

If you are planning to take out a mortgage that allows you to make a relatively small down payment (of less than 20 percent), you should be aware that your lender is likely to insist that you purchase Private Mortgage Insurance (PMI) to protect him. You will pay for this insurance with a small increase in your monthly payments and it protects the lender in case you default on your payments.

Here is a list of the closing costs you may expect to face.

Mortgage Fees—
    Loan origination fee (or assumption fee)
    "Points" or loan discount fee*
    Document preparation fee
    Appraisal fee
    Credit report fee
    Inspection fee
    Collection set-up fee
    Impound set-up/service fee

---

* You may want to pay these charges by separate check to the lender rather than having them deducted from the loan proceeds. At this writing, if you do that when you purchase a home, the entire sum you pay for points is tax deductible in the year you pay it. If it is deducted from the loan proceeds, you have to amortize the figure over the life of the loan. Check with your tax advisor for current status of this tax benefit.

Insurance—
> Hazard Insurance
> Mortgage Insurance
> Home Warranty

Taxes—
> Prorated annual property taxes for city & county
> Transfer taxes (if applicable)

Attorney—
> Fees to review documents, render advice and assist in closing escrow

Title Fees—
> Title search
> Title insurance
> Document preparation
> Notary and other fees

Recording and Transfer Fees—
> Recording fee for deed
> Recording fee for mortgage
> Recording fee for releases

Miscellaneous—
> Pest inspection and report
> Structural inspection and report
> Inspection of extra systems (i.e., pool, etc.)

Affordable Ways To "Get Down"

One of the axioms of life is that two can live more cheaply than one—and that this can make it easier for a couple to save a down payment. But when it comes to accessing other ways to handle the down payment, you are their equal. (And if your income is less than the household income of some of your married friends, that may actually help you in some programs! More on that later in Chapter 5.)

All In The Family

The old tried and true method is to get help accumulating your down payment from relatives, but that has some pitfalls. If you structure it as a loan, most lenders will include it in your total indebtedness when considering you for a mortgage. To avoid this, your relatives will need to give you the money and supply a "gift letter" to your lender.

If you are thinking about having a private loan agreement on the side, think twice. Your lender is likely to consider this fraud if the agreement comes to light—say if you default and your relative decides to sue. If your relatives are able to make a gift, they should talk with their financial advisor about potential tax advantages they may be eligible for.

Divorce Special

If you have been married before and owned a house with your spouse, you may have special reasons to buy a home right now. If you received funds in a property settlement or divorce settlement that came from the sale of your marital home, current tax law gives you between two years before and two years after the sale of the marital home to buy a replacement home if you want to defer taxes on all that money.

Simply, if you and your husband sold a home worth $200,000 and split the proceeds 50/50, you would need to buy a personal residence worth at least $100,000 within the two-year period or plan to give Uncle Sam a big hunk of the money you received. You are not required to use all the money you received in the divorce to buy the replacement home—you can take out a large mortgage and keep the cash for other uses. This is especially attractive if you can qualify for a large new mortgage and want to maintain your cash liquidity while gaining the tax benefits of a mortgage. If you believe you may be in this position, talk to your tax advisor about your personal situation.

Equity Sharing

Another way of handling the down payment problem is equity sharing. This is a technique that matches a savings-poor but otherwise well-qualified buyer (you) with an investor who puts up most or all of the down payment. At the end of the term of the agreement (usually three to five years), you can sell the home and split the appreciation according to the formula in your contract, refinance the home and return the investor's original investment and share of appreciation, or sell to the investor and take your profits. If you sell the property or let the investor buy you out, you can defer taxes on your gain by investing it in the purchase of another home under IRS Code 1034.

There are several great advantages to equity sharing. One is that during the contract, you may receive the tax advantages of home ownership (often according to your percentage of ownership in the property).

Then after a few years, you are likely to receive enough from the sale to enable you to buy another home on your own. This is called leveraging. With your small investment up front (of about five percent) and your payments toward the mortgage (you would probably be paying about as much in rent anyway), you can control a portion—often half—of a valuable investment, your home.

When you are negotiating the equity sharing contract, you may want to have an experienced Realtor, tax advisor and/or lawyer advising you since there are so many variables. A simple arrangement could have the investor make a one-time investment in exchange for a portion of the appreciation in value (often 50 percent) leaving you responsible for the mortgage payments and any repairs and remodeling done during the contract period. More complex arrangements could have provisions for dividing costs of any expensive remodeling projects or for adjusting the shares of the appreciation in value to reflect each party's contributions of cash and/or labor.

For more information about the details of equity sharing, you may want to read *The Equity Sharing Book* by Diana Bull and Elaine St. James. This helpful manual should be available through your local bookstore.

Lease Option

For Jeannie Peterson, lease option was the key to buying her own home. She knew she wanted a yard to putter in and the privacy of a detached, single-family home, but she did not have a large down payment.

In a lease option, you lease the home and usually pay an "option fee" which gives you the right to buy the home during a specific time frame for a price which was agreed on in the beginning. You live in the house and pay rent. Often the rent is higher than prevailing rates and some or all of the rent you pay may be applied to your down payment, if you take up your option and purchase the home.

Peterson says one of the potential pitfalls she did not understand going into her contract was that if she could not complete the deal, she stood to lose her deposit (option fee). She says now that if she were to do it again, she would try for a clause in the contract which would allow her to get back her initial deposit, but forfeit the extra rent payments.

The possibility of forfeiting your option fee and extra rent are more than balanced for many buyers by the chance to get in with a low down payment, buy the home a year or two later at today's price (especially attractive in markets where homes are appreciating well), and spend time in the home discovering whether the neighborhood and lifestyle are really what you want.

Lease options can also be just what you need if you want to buy a home now, but can't because you need to pay off some other existing debt (like charge accounts or car payments) to improve your debt-to-income ratio so you can qualify for a mortgage. Again, while you are improving your credit rating, you are contributing to your down payment as part of your monthly rental, and you have tied down the price of the home, even if the market goes up dramatically.

One caution though, unless your contract calls for the seller to finance the whole mortgage, you will be especially smart to pre-qualify for a loan before making your deposit. Don't count on good luck or dropping interest rates to help you get a mortgage when the lease option agreement matures.

Peterson, who did not prequalify, warns that one thing she had not anticipated was the stress while she was arranging financing. She knew that if the deal fell through, she not only lost a potential investment, she would lose her home. She says, "It was a real emotional burden, not knowing if I would have a home next month."

You will find that lease options are most likely to be offered in a stable market where the seller does not expect the property to appreciate dramatically during the lease. However, other times the seller may be motivated by wanting to sell the property now, but keep the tax advantages a little longer until you exercise your option.

One example might be a seller who wants to qualify for the "Over 55" $125,000 exclusion of gain on his taxes, but he is not quite age 55 yet. You may be able to arrange to buy the home under a lease option and close the sale next year, after the seller's 55th birthday. That way, he has a renter who is very motivated to take good care of the home and in all probability who will buy it and it may allow him to move on with his career or retirement plans.

Special Programs

If your income is modest and you have had problems saving a down payment, there may be a special program in your area which can help. Some of these involve very low down payment, low interest rate bond programs to help first-time buyers or people willing to buy in targeted areas. Other programs offer special benefits if you are willing to provide labor on building or renovating your home through a "sweat equity" arrangement. To find out about local programs, talk to local lenders, real estate agents, and call your state's Department of Housing or its equivalent. Your library or the office of your state representative can tell you where to call—or start by calling the number listed for your state in Appendix I.

Buy With A Friend

Buying a house with a friend can be the best answer for some people. It allows you to pool your incomes and down payments which is likely to help you both live in a more attractive area than either of you could afford individually.

Before you buy, you and your friend should talk about your expectations with each other and a lawyer. A good partnership agreement—in writing—can prevent a lot of problems in the future. Some of the topics you need to decide on include:

- How will the ownership be vested, as tenants in common or joint tenants? If as tenants in common, will it be 50/50, or will one person's contribution entitle them to a larger share? How will the tax benefits be divided?

- Who will be responsible for paying for what? Paying the mortgage payment may seem simple, but then who decides who pays for necessary vs. desired repairs and remodeling? You should be very specific in your contract or specific laws may control these factors.
- If there is a disagreement about how things are to be handled, how will a decision be made? Again, the law may have a rule that applies unless you both agree on your own arrangements.
- If one partner marries, dies, or just decides to leave, what happens? Your lender may want to have some input on this topic. After all, you may both remain liable for the loan, even though one goes off the title.
- Do you want to have house rules about personal concerns like how many days or weeks guests can stay?

As you can see, there are many techniques you can use to help you get more house than you may have thought you could qualify for. There are even more programs in Chapter 5 if you have not owned a home before (or at least not lately). The key factors are finding the right professional lenders and Realtors while keeping an open but critical mind to the creative opportunities available to you.

And remember, even if the first home you buy is not your dream house, no one says you have to stay there for 30 years. In a few years, you are likely to be making more money. That, coupled with the appreciation in value in your home, will enable you to move to an even nicer home.

4

All Home Loans Are Not Created Equal

A generation ago, the fixed-rate mortgage was pretty much the standard. However, today you have a virtual smorgasbord of financing options available to you.

Kinds Of Lenders

As you begin to look for a mortgage, you will find that there are two basic kinds of lenders. Some are called mortgage brokers and others are mortgage bankers.

Mortgage Brokers

A mortgage broker may be a firm or individual who matches borrowers and investors and is paid a fee for that service by either the investor or the borrower. Once the loan is made, a broker does not service it (services include collecting the payments and disbursing funds to the investor, taxing entities and hazard insurance companies). The broker may work with many investors offering hundreds of programs. Since each investor establishes his own criteria for credit, property and income, a mortgage broker can almost always match a borrower with a program that suits his needs.

A good mortgage broker can save you time and energy by doing the research for you once she knows what you need. You can find a good mortgage broker through referrals from your real estate agent or friends who have worked with her. You can check on the professional status of the broker with a quick call to your state licensing department which sets the standards for mortgage brokers. It is also a good sign if she or he is a member of the National Association of Mortgage Brokers which is based in Phoenix, Arizona, as members receive continual educational opportunities and adhere to a strict code of Business Ethics.

One problem some people have faced after using a mortgage broker is that the broker handles the details of the loan origination, but once approved, the servicing of that loan is taken over by the lender or a servicer hired by the lender. Sometimes the company that services your loan will change and you will need to send your payments to a new address.

Normally, changing servicers is just an inconvenience. Unfortunately, there are some scam artists out there who will get names and other information about loans and then send you a letter saying they are servicing your loan now and you should send your payments directly to them.

WATCH OUT!

The scam artists have no intention of using the money you send them to pay your mortgage. They will be gone before you know what happened and your mortgage will be in arrears. If anyone sends you a letter telling you to send your mortgage payments to them and you have not gotten a letter from your old mortgage servicer notifying you of the change, phone (and write a back-up letter to) your old mortgage servicer immediately.

If the change is genuine, your current servicer should send you confirmation in writing. If the change is a scam, your current servicer will tell you to keep making your normal payments and may provide information on what steps you may be able to take to help stop the people who are attempting to defraud you. Fortunately, this scam is not likely to happen to you, but you should always be cautious if you are notified to mail your payments somewhere new.

Mortgage Banker

The mortgage banker, on the other hand, does service the loans she makes. She will collect your monthly payments, forward the proceeds to the investors who have purchased the loan, maintain escrow accounts for payment of taxes and insurance and act as the investors' representative if a problem should arise with your loan (such as default). The mortgage banker earns her income through origination and servicing fees on the loans she makes.

The mortgage banker will often borrow money from a bank to make the loans. Once she has made your loan, she will pool it with other mortgages and sell it to investors on the secondary market. The proceeds received from the secondary market are used to repay the bank loan, and the process starts over.

There is another kind of mortgage banker you should also be aware of. This is a portfolio lender. These mortgage bankers hold onto the loans they make rather than selling them on the secondary market. Monthly payments made by previous buyers create a source of funds for future loans.

Portfolio lenders can be especially helpful if you have problems meeting the borrowing ratios explained in Chapter 3. Because these lenders are not going to sell your loan on the secondary market, they may not always hold you to the same qualifying ratios as lenders who do sell the loans might. They can also be helpful if you have other specialized needs that other lenders are not interested in meeting.

There are about 100 different mortgage banking associations across the country which serve their members at the local and state level. Membership in one of these is likely to be an indicator that a mortgage banker is interested in aiming for high professional goals. There is also the Mortgage Bankers Association of America, which is based in Washington, D.C., and has about 2,800 member firms and corporations.

Kinds Of Loans

As you consider the variety of loan types available to you, evaluate them in respect to your personal needs.

For instance, if your career is stable, like a teacher, plumber, lawyer or police officer, you may be planning to buy one home and live there for twenty years. In that case, a fixed-rate mortgage can supply the predictability and peace of mind you want.

On the other hand, if you are in a profession where you move frequently—or you are buying your first home and expect to move up in a few years—an adjustable-rate mortgage (especially one with a low introductory interest rate) may be more attractive.

Fixed-Rate Mortgage

The FIXED-RATE mortgage is a comfortable standard in the industry. It allows you to know exactly what the payments for principal and interest will be every month for the length of the loan. When the interest rates are low, it is especially attractive because you can tie down that rate regardless of what happens to the economy. When rates are high, a fixed-rate mortgage is much less likely to be attractive.

The fixed-rate mortgage is mostly seen in 30- and 15-year contracts. The longer length allows for smaller payments, but the shorter term allows you to own your home free and clear sooner while substantially reducing the total amount of interest paid to the lender over the life of the loan. You may also get an interest break by going for the shorter term.

As an example, take a mortgage for $80,000. If you were to take out a fixed-rate mortgage for 30 years at 10 percent, you can expect to pay $835 per month for principal and interest. Over the life of the loan, you will pay in excess of $172,000 in interest. On the other hand, if you went for the shorter 15-year term (and your lender gave you a half-percentage rate break for reducing their risk) your figures would be very different. Your monthly payment would rise to $969, but over the life of the loan, you would save more than $100,000 in interest payments.

One drawback to a fixed-rate mortgage is that lenders tend to have more stringent qualifying standards for it, reducing the number of people who are able to qualify. Also, since the payments for a 15-year loan can be up to 20 percent higher than for the 30-year loan, it is even more difficult to qualify for.

Adjustable-Rate Mortgage

An ADJUSTABLE-RATE MORTGAGE (ARM) typically offers a lower initial interest rate which remains stable until the first adjustment date (which was defined in your contract). At the adjustment date, the interest rate—and the resulting monthly payment—can be raised or lowered depending on the performance of the index your loan is based on.

The index is the published measure of interest rates on certain types of borrowing or investments. One typical index is the 11th District Cost of Funds. The index is then added to a pre-specified surcharge called the "margin" which covers the lender's costs for servicing the loan.

One feature of an ARM you should be especially interested in is the cap.

There are two basic kinds of caps. The first is an interest rate cap which can either limit the maximum yearly increase on the interest rate, or set a maximum interest rate for the life of the loan.

The second cap is a payment cap which limits the increase on monthly or yearly payments. The important thing you should be aware of with a payment cap is that if the interest rate goes up to the point that the payment would be larger than the cap allows, the excess interest due will not be forgiven, it will be deferred. This deferred interest is also known as negative amortization. Any deferred interest will be added to the unpaid loan balance. You could conceivably end up owing more for your house when you sell it than you paid for it originally!

Some ARM's are available with a convertible feature. At the buyer's option, the mortgage can be converted to a fixed-rate loan during a time period specified in the contract.

The primary benefit of ARM's is that they normally allow you to qualify for a larger loan than you could obtain in a fixed-rate loan. The initial (qualifying) rate is likely to be lower and the lender is likely to allow a higher percentage of your gross income for housing expenses with an ARM. The drawback is that if interest rates soar like they did in the early 1980's, you could be facing dramatically higher home payments at some future time when it is impossible for you to refinance with an attractive fixed-rate mortgage. On the other hand, you may get lucky and have your rates go down (if your contract allows). However, if interest rates do go down, you may want to refinance with a fixed-rate loan that protects you from potential interest increases in the future.

There may also be a variation on the ARM available which involves a fixed-rate mortgage that has a fixed rate for a period of time and then adjustments to current market rates at one or more pre-set times in the future.

FHA

The FHA loan is probably the one of the best known American mortgages. This remarkable tool enables buyers to purchase a home with as little as 3 percent down. Traditionally, FHA interest rates are lower than conventional rates, and there are a variety of mortgage instruments you can access with an FHA loan.

Also, 30-year fixed-rate mortgages are frequently available through FHA lenders even when some conventional lenders only want to offer adjustable-rate mortgages because of the uncertainty in the marketplace.

FHA also offers graduated payment mortgages and adjustable-rate mortgages. These instruments offer you a lower initial payment rate—and the FHA graduated payment program allows some buyers to qualify for up to $30,000 higher loan amounts because of the greatly reduced first year payment. The reason this works is because you will be qualified for the loan on the basis of your first year payment alone.

If you are looking at resale homes, you may want to keep an eye out for those which currently have FHA loans originally made before

December 1, 1986, because these loans are fully assumable. You could assume (or take over) these loans without having to qualify or pay new buyer's costs. You can cover the purchase costs beyond the amount of the assumed mortgage by using second mortgages or contracts for deed. A benefit to the seller is that he does not have to worry about the house appraising for the sale price, since no appraisal is required.

FHA loans made after December 1, 1986, have a partial "due on sale" clause that requires qualification if the loan is assumed during the first two years or two years after a subsequent assumption. FHA loans made after December 15, 1989, require qualification on the assumption and may not be assumed by investors.

However, as a buyer, you should be aware that some sellers and real estate agents prefer not to sell their home to buyers seeking new FHA loans. This attitude stems from past appraisals done by FHA staff appraisers who often came in with values less than the sale price and included extensive repair requirements. FHA now uses independent appraisers which has eliminated many of these problems.

If a lack of time is a problem, then applying for an FHA loan may be too. Normal FHA processing time is 4–6 weeks, compared to 2–4 weeks for conventional financing. However, many FHA lenders are now approved for automatic loan approvals which can substantially speed up your processing.

FHA loans come in a variety of plans to suit different needs. Some of the options you might want to pursue include the 15- and 30-year fixed-rate loans, adjustable-rate and graduated payment loans, and growing equity programs that allow you to gradually increase your payments to pay off the loan early and build equity faster.

VA Mortgages

The VETERANS or VA loan can be a godsend if you are eligible to take advantage of this program. These loans are often made with *NO DOWN PAYMENT* at all, and frequently offer lower interest rates than ordinarily available with other kinds of loans.

Actually, the VA does not make loans directly, it guarantees loans made by other lenders like mortgage companies, savings and loan institutions, or banks. The VA guarantee means that the lender is protected against loss if you are not able to make the payments. In practice, the guarantee encourages lenders to offer qualified veterans more favorable terms on their loan.

The amount of the guarantee depends on the loan amount and whether the veteran has used some entitlement before. With the current guarantee, a veteran who has not previously used the benefit may be eligible to obtain a VA guaranteed loan up to $184,000 depending on his or her income level and the appraised value of the property.

The controlling detail is your eligibility. Veterans with at least 90 days active duty service, and a discharge that was not dishonorable, during WWII and later periods, are eligible. The time frames are for WWII (9/16/40–7/25/47), Korean conflict (6/27/50–1/31/55), and Vietnam era (8/5/64–5/7/75). More recently, reservists and National Guard members who were activated on or after August 2, 1990, for the Persian Gulf Conflict and who served at least 90 days and were discharged honorably are also eligible. If you have any questions about your eligibility, your local VA office can help you.

Veterans with service only during peacetime periods and active duty military personnel must have had more than 180 days of active service. Veterans of enlisted service beginning after September 7, 1980, or officers with service beginning after October 16, 1981, must, in most cases, have served at least two years.

The flexibility of the VA loan is wonderful. You can use it to buy a detached home, townhouse or condominium in a VA-approved project. You can even use it to build a home of your dreams. If you fall in love with an older home that needs restoration, you can use the money to buy and improve the home. You can use the funds to improve your home, including the installation of a solar heating and/or cooling system or other weatherization improvements. You can even use the proceeds to buy a factory-built home and/or lot.

If you believe you may be eligible for a VA guaranteed loan, the first step is to apply for a Certificate of Eligibility at your local VA office on VA Form 26-1880.

Next, you decide on a home and sign a purchase agreement (if you need the VA guarantee to complete the transaction, you definitely want to consider making your approval for the VA loan a condition of the sales agreement).

Then, you arrange for an appraisal to be ordered by the VA. Most regional offices offer a "speed-up" telephone appraisal system. Call your local VA office for details.

Now you apply to a mortgage lender for the loan.

When the loan commitment has been issued, you close escrow and move in!

While there is no VA requirement for a down payment (probably the best deal going these days), there are some minor costs associated with a VA mortgage. A funding fee of up to 1.25 percent must be paid to the VA by all but certain exempt veterans. But, if you have even a small down payment of 5–10 percent, that fee will be reduced.

However, regardless of the customary procedures in your area, no commission or brokerage fee may be charged to a veteran buyer under this program. Reasonable closing costs may be charged by the lender, but they may not be included in your loan. Under some specific conditions, veterans also may be charged with points on their loan.

If you have any questions about your eligibility or how the VA loans may help you, call your local VA office which should be listed in your telephone book under U.S. Government.

Comparing Loans

Because of the incredible variety of loans available, it will help to set out the specifics of each loan on the chart on page 50 to compare the options available to you.

If you are only looking at fixed-rate mortgages, not all the questions will apply.

Loan Program Comparisons

LENDER QUESTION	LOAN 1	LOAN 2	LOAN 3	LOAN 4
1. Loan type				
2. Initial interest rate				
3. Term in years				
4. Lender fees (points)				
5. Prepayment penalty				
6. Co-borrowers O.K.?				
7. Max. annual negative amortization				
8. Assumable?				
9. Which index used?				
10. When is margin set?				
11. Frequency of interest rate adjustments				
12. Frequency of payment adjustments				
13. Interest rate caps				
14. What period covered by caps				
15. Against what interest rate is cap increased?				
16. Are there payment increase caps?				
17. How much/How long?				
18. Do interest and payment caps apply to up and down interest moves?				
19. Does index look to most recent change or the average?				
20. Initial payment				

**This chart is adapted from *The Equity Sharing Book*
by Diana Bull and Elaine St. James. Used with their permission.**

Impounds Impact Your Budget

When you are talking to lenders, the word "impound" will undoubtedly come up. Simply put, impounds are funds paid by you and held by the lender in a special account to pay your home taxes and/or hazard insurance.

If you are getting a mortgage for more than 80 percent of the price of the home, your lender is likely to require that you pay a monthly sum into an impound account. This will be done by adding the amount of impound to your monthly mortgage payment. Other lenders may require impound accounts for different reasons.

The reason for impound accounts is that the lender is trying to protect its investment. By collecting and disbursing the tax funds, the lender protects itself from the possibility of the borrower defaulting on his property taxes. When that happens, the property tax lien takes legal precedence over the mortgage lien, threatening the lender's security. To protect their position and give an incentive to borrowers to accept an impound account, some lenders will offer better terms like a reduction in loan fees or a minor break on the interest rate.

As a consumer, you may prefer to use an impound account because it protects you from having to come up with large sums of money when the property tax and hazard insurance bills come due. On the other hand, if you are good at budgeting your funds, you may prefer to manage your own tax and insurance payments and keep control of the money until you actually have to pay the bills.

Watch Out For Surprises

Surprises were the last thing Stephen Risner wanted when he bought his home. He even got a fixed-rate mortgage so there would not be any changes in the size of his home payments. But he did not count on changes in the amount his lender charged for his impound accounts to cover his taxes and insurance.

Not long after he bought, his lender informed him that his impound account was underfunded and they were adjusting his monthly payment up $45 per month. Risner admits that he had stretched his budget to the limit to make the purchase and the increase was a bit of a hardship. Later, when he talked to his co-workers, he found that others had had the same problem.

He speculates that the original amounts that were charged may have been estimated at the lowest possible figure to help him qualify for his loan, but he wishes that he had known what his real costs would be up front.

In all fairness, if you have an impound account, the amount you contribute to it each year may be changed because of changes (let's face it, increases) in the costs of taxes and insurance.

The Lure Of The Bi-Weekly Mortgage Payment

The siren song of ways to save money is rarely sweeter than when someone shows you how much money you can expect to save over the life of your mortgage by making bi-weekly payments.

The theory is simple. Instead of making 12 monthly payments a year, you make a half payment every two weeks. This tends to work well for people who are paid weekly but may be difficult for people who have predictable monthly incomes and who will have problems during the months they have to make three of these payments.

Over the period of a year, payments made on a bi-weekly basis add up to the same amount as 13 monthly payments. The benefit is that on a 30-year $100,000 fixed-rate loan, you can expect to save more than $55,000 over the life of the loan and have your mortgage paid off roughly eight years early.

Do It Yourself

If this sounds good to you, the easiest way to do it is to open a separate bank account (preferably interest bearing) and put your bi-weekly payment in the account. Then, once a month, use the money to pay your mortgage. You can send in the extra half payments as they occur. When you send in the extra money, note on your payment slip that the money is to be applied to the outstanding principal.

If you have a predictable monthly income and pulling out an extra half payment some months would be a hardship, you can still get the same benefit. Figure out what one-twelfth of your payment is.

Then increase your monthly payment by that amount (with instructions to your lender to apply the excess to your principal).

The beauty of both of these methods is that if you decide you need that month's excess payment for another purpose, that's fine.

On the other hand, do not think that by paying your mortgage ahead of time, you can skip a month if you feel like it. The terms of your mortgage probably prohibit that. So before you worry about accelerating your mortgage payments with bi-weekly payments you should have several months payments in the bank in case a problem comes up.

If you prefer a more structured arrangement for your bi-weekly mortgage payment, many stock brokers, insurance agents and financial planners offer plans as do some mortgage banks. When you choose to go this route, be sure to ask how and how much the provider is paid for giving the service.

Watch Your Wallet

In her nationally syndicated column, Jane Bryant Quinn warns that independent agents who offer this service may or may not have your best interests at heart. She mentions one Delaware company that instructed prospects not to check with their bank about the firm because bankers are greedy and would not want you to save the interest on your mortgage. As Quinn quickly points out, your bank may be able to suggest ways you could save even more money, like using a 15-year mortgage.

You will also be paying for this service. Quinn quotes rates of anywhere from $50 plus a per transaction charge of $2.50 to $500 or more plus a transaction charge. If you simply handled the payments yourself, you would have that much more to apply to your principal—and your mortgage would be paid off even sooner.

Perhaps the most important point Quinn raises about independent agents who offer to handle bi-weekly mortgage payments for you is that when you agree to their plan, they get the ability to dip into your bank account. Some shady companies have simply taken the money and disappeared, leaving the client with an unpaid mortgage.

5

Special Help For First-Timers

While it is rarely easy to buy a home, being single can bring its own challenges to the equation. The primary problems tend to be inability to save a down payment since you are your sole support and inability to qualify for a traditional mortgage since you only have one income in a society where it frequently takes two to earn enough to cover mortgage payments.

But there is help for each of these problems. Sometimes programs can even be combined to address both problems at the same time.

Mortgage Revenue Bonds

One of the best known programs is the Mortgage Revenue Bond (MRB) program which is available nationally (although Kansas issues its MRB's at the local level). According to the National Council of State Housing Agencies, the MRB program is the only federal program available to reduce mortgage costs for lower income, first-time home buyers whose income is otherwise inadequate to purchase a home.

This program is designed to help people who work hard, but whose jobs do not pay high wages. To qualify, you can earn 100 percent or less of the applicable median family income (115 percent if you have two dependents besides yourself), and buy a principal residence that does not exceed 90 percent of the average area home purchase price.

The median family income will vary depending on where you live. Your state Housing Finance Agency (listed with phone numbers in Appendix I) can tell you what the figures are in your area. You may be surprised how high your income can be and still qualify. Also, if you are interested in buying an existing home in a targeted area (where the agency is trying to encourage home ownership), your income and sales price limits may be higher than the agency would normally allow you.

In practice, state Housing Finance Agencies provide MRB loans to people or families whose incomes averaged only 75.6 percent of median income. In 1991, the average income of an MRB borrower was $28,740, compared with $43,900 for the average conventional first-time buyer, $51,400 for all conventional home buyers, and $38,000 for the median U.S. household.

On a statewide average, the household income varied from a low of $21,309 in Tennessee to $40,192 in Connecticut. The average prices statewide of the homes purchased were highest in Hawaii, where the average purchase price was $112,565.

Even then, certain high-priced areas may still allow for purchasing more expensive homes. For example, in San Francisco, the sales price limit at this writing is $203,400 and the single buyer can qualify with an income of up to $59,900—hardly a modest income for most single people.

MRB's are normally only available to people who are first-time buyers *or* have not owned a home within the last three years. Again, that may be negotiable if you are interested in a home in a targeted area.

Along with their basic programs, many state programs offer customized opportunities to target particular housing needs and population groups. Housing Finance Agencies reserve portions of their funds (called set asides) for particular kinds of first-time buyers like single parents, minorities, and very low income persons. If you don't fit in those categories, you may get special consideration for buying government-held foreclosed homes, rehabilitated homes or newly constructed homes in targeted areas.

You will not get the loan directly through your state agency; the people there will refer you to local lenders who are participating in the program.

Before you write off the idea of living in a targeted area thinking the homes there may be less desirable, get your state agency to tell you where those areas are and have a real estate agent show you around them. You may be surprised to find areas that are being revitalized and where your property values are likely to appreciate handsomely in the next few years.

Because the tax-exempt bonds used to finance this program give investors a lower rate of return than taxable bonds, the Housing Finance Agencies issuing the bonds can lend the proceeds to home buyers at interest rates as much as 2.5 percent below conventional rates, with substantial monthly savings to the borrower.

In addition to their MRB programs, state Housing Finance Agencies may (depending on the state) offer specialized housing programs which are designed to target specific needs or population groups. The kinds of programs you may find in your state include:

1. Home improvement loans, including loans to repair substandard homes, to rehabilitate houses, and to finance energy conservation/energy efficient improvements;
2. Lease/purchase arrangements, under which renters are provided the opportunity to eventually purchase their unit;
3. Incentives to promote the construction of lower-priced homes;
4. Loans and other assistance to help lower income households purchase foreclosed homes from the Resolution Trust Corporation, Veterans Administration, and Department of Housing and Urban Development;
5. Manufactured housing loans;
6. Emergency mortgage assistance which provides funds to newly unemployed homeowners to help them make their mortgage payments and keep their homes until they can get back on their feet again; and
7. Credit counseling.

Sweat Equity And Down Payment Programs

There are two other programs possibly available to you through your state Housing Finance Agency that deserve special attention.

First is "sweat equity" assistance. This program counts the value of your labor in helping build your home as down payment toward the purchase price. A group of home buyers works together on building a set of homes, one for each represented household.

The work can be hard, and you may be required to spend a substantial amount of your free time over many months to help build your home and others in your neighborhood, but you do not have to be a construction professional to participate.

Building the neighborhood together can be a great way to get into a brand new home and really get to know your neighbors at the same time. The work you do will be supervised by professionals, and some complex technical areas like plumbing and electrical wiring may be contracted out if there are no licensed professionals working with you.

You're Not Down And Out—You're Down And In!

If you have had a problem saving a down payment, you should absolutely ask your state Housing Finance Agency about special programs to help with the down payment and closing costs. Usually, these programs offer assistance in the form of a deferred payment, or no or low interest second mortgages on your home.

These MRB programs are well received by American home-owners. In fact, more than 1.3 million home buyers have benefitted directly from MRB loans. If a below market-rate interest, fixed-rate loan sounds good to you, call your state agency (remember, Appendix I) today. The few cents you spend on the phone call could make it possible for you to be comfortably at home in your own place before you know it.

Mortgage Credit Certificates

A 1984 tax law created the Mortgage Credit Certificate (MCC) program to provide state and local issuers with an alternative to mortgage bonds to assist first-time buyers. Since then, there has been a uniquely different way for you to benefit from home ownership.

If you qualify, MCC's can provide you with a non-refundable federal income tax credit. That credit can be used for a specified percentage of the annual interest you pay on a mortgage to finance the purchase, qualified home improvement, or qualified rehabilitation of your home. MCC's may be used with loans on single-family homes, condominiums, and cooperative homes, and certain manufactured (mobile) homes.

When you get a Certificate, it should specify the credit rate and principal amount of your mortgage. Depending on factors unique to your personal situation, you may be eligible for a tax credit of up to 20 percent of the interest you pay on your mortgage loan every year. While the annual credit amount you may claim is no more than $2,000, under specific circumstances, you may be able to carry forward unused credit for up to three taxable years.

Motivation = Success

David Durbin heartily recommends the MCC programs. He used one to enable him to buy his home in Fayette County, Kentucky, with only three percent down. Durbin really wanted a home of his own. In fact, he had given up his apartment and arranged his work schedule so he was out of town, living in motels, for almost nine months so he could save a down payment.

He admits that during that time, he really missed having an active personal life, since having a social life had come to mean spending the weekend on a friend's sofa. His clothes hung on a rod in the back seat of his car and his furniture was scattered everywhere from his brother's garage to his parents' basement. Durbin even got rid of all his old pans, silverware, etc., in anticipation of his new home. He wanted everything to be as special and new as his home would be.

As difficult as it was, all his sacrifice paid off.

59

Durbin was the first person to move into his newly constructed neighborhood. He now owns a beautiful, 1,300 square foot, single-family brick home with vaulted ceilings. Restful views of a lake are visible from out back.

Durbin is thrilled with his purchase as an investment and a home. On two sides of his neighborhood there are single-family homes that are much more expensive. He anticipates that the appreciation on those homes will help his home gain value quickly, offering him an attractive return on his investment if he decides to sell.

Local Programs Tackle Local Problems

Throughout the country, there are grassroots programs set up to help people buy a home they might otherwise never have. One outstanding program is based in New Orleans.

The problem was obvious in New Orleans. Roughly 70 percent of the residents in most neighborhoods across the country are home-owners; that same percentage were renters in New Orleans. Much of this large stock of rental housing was deteriorating because of absentee landlords, further decreasing the quality of life for the people who stayed.

Recognizing that home ownership was the key to revitalizing the city, John and Holly Pavy DeBlois, a wealthy local couple, founded the New Orleans' Neighborhood Development Foundation (NDF) to help people buy homes.

But this is no give-away. Using the theory that it is better to teach someone to fish than just give him a meal, NDF teaches the participants how to fish—and then gives them a pole to help them get started.

Each applicant must pass an initial screening. To be eligible for NDF's services, clients must have incomes which fall generally within HUD's low (80 percent of median) and very low (50 percent of median) ranges, stable employment, established credit histories, and the ability to put at least $1,500 toward the cost of purchasing a home.

Since NDF places heavy emphasis on self-sufficiency and the judicious use of personal resources, clients must become active participants in the process of home ownership, and they are required to attend a 12-hour course of instruction in family budget management, working with real estate agents, home selection, home financing, home maintenance, and the rights, privileges and responsibilities of ownership.

NDF stays with the client after training and acts as an advocate, counselor, and advisor for each client throughout the entire purchase process—everything from searching for appropriate homes to closing the sale.

Clients are also helped with below-market rate financing through the New Orleans Home Mortgage Authority, Louisiana Housing Finance Agency, and some local lenders.

Is it working? Since 1986, nearly 1,500 families have completed the home buyer training program. Over five hundred clients have purchased homes on the open market representing about $25,000,000 in permanent financing. The typical buyer has an income of about $17,350 and buys a home for about $40,000. Another 600+ have pre-qualified for permanent financing and are at various stages in their home search.

A Success Story

Denise Perez is not looking any more. Three years ago, this nurse at the University of New Orleans bought the home she had dreamed of all her life.

As a divorced mother of two sons, Perez lived in a rental, convinced that home ownership was beyond her grasp. But then, the personnel department at work circulated a brochure about the Neighborhood Development Foundation. Perez put it away with some other papers, but the idea began germinating in her mind. Months later, she decided to give it a try.

First she went to some traditional home lenders in her area, but she could not qualify financially with any of them. Then she remembered the brochure about NDF and dug it out.

Within a day of calling NDF she had qualified for the program. Soon she started the course. Then, a few weeks into the course she found it—her dream home—complete with a swimming pool, cabana, and patio with a double grill, wet bar, and refrigerator.

There was only one problem. The sellers had already accepted an offer on the house. Then that offer fell through, and Perez started to dare to hope, but she told the sellers that she could not possibly make an offer until she finished the course and was qualified for the low-cost financing.

So she held her breath a little and said a few prayers.

Then another potential buyer signed a contract on the home and gave the sellers substantial earnest money to hold the deal. The sellers called Perez sadly to tell her, and Perez tried to remain cheerful when she reminded them that she had no right to a claim on the home since she was not able to make an offer yet, and she wished them well in the sale.

Then that sale fell through two days before Perez was to finish her course and be able to make an offer. This time, the sellers called and said they would not even try to sell it to anyone else until she could meet with them—since it certainly appeared that *Someone* wanted her to have that house.

Perez even told them her bad news, that while the asking price was $65,000, she had only been able to qualify for enough financing to purchase a home for $55,000. Recalling that someone had given them a break when they bought their first home (and now they were ready to retire), they met her price and the home is hers. She even found that affording the new payments was not too much of a stretch. Her housing payments went up $50 per month from what she paid in rent and because of the warm weather and frequent rains, her utilities only went up about $5.40 per month, even with the pool.

Now, after a long day at work, she comes home and jumps into that pool. Her sons bring their friends home, and her yard is a popular gathering place for family and neighbors (whom she is quick to remind to bring their own towels).

Perez notes that the training she received was instrumental in helping her buy her home. Before the classes, she was somewhat intimidated by the jargon the lenders used. But in her training, she learned that any time she does not understand something being said, she has the right to insist that the speaker stop and explain the term to her in a way she can understand. She found that very empowering as a single woman dealing with a complex transaction.

And . . .

As you are considering programs offered by governmental agencies to encourage home purchases, remember to look into the non-government-based special opportunities like NDF in your community too, and talk with your real estate agent about concepts like lease-option which was mentioned in Chapter 3.

For the most part, if you are making enough money to rent a comfortable apartment and your credit is good, you will be able to buy a home one way or another. Talk to state agencies, local lenders, and real estate agents to find out what programs will best suit your needs.

6

Be A Star—Get
An Agent!

Why Get An Agent?

Unless you are already a real estate broker or lawyer, you should probably get an agent to help you find a home and handle the seemingly endless stream of forms you have to wade through to buy that home. A good agent can help you find a house, negotiate the sale, search out lenders who best suit your needs, and smooth your way through the process. He or she can also help you find experienced, qualified professionals you may choose to hire for everything from inspecting the roof to repairing the plumbing.

While you may feel that using a real estate agent will restrict you to looking at resale homes, that is not necessarily true. If you want to look at newly built housing, it can be helpful to have an agent working as a Buyer's Broker (as described later in this chapter) to advise you. When you are dealing with the salespeople at a new development, those salespeople work for the developer. As pleasant and helpful as they are, their primary loyalty is to the developer. Especially if you are not an experienced home buyer, you may want to have an expert in your corner who can advise you on everything from negotiating strategy to the advisability of impartial inspections.

In some areas, especially during down markets, some developers will even advertise that they invite "Broker participation." Under that condition, they may even pay for your agent's fees—but be careful. If their goal is to make your agent a sub-agent of the seller's agent as described below in "Kinds of Representation," then you may still want to hire a Buyer's Broker agent whose first responsibility will be to protect your interests.

If you are looking at homes sporting "For Sale By Owner" signs, you may also want to hire a buyer's agent to help you and look out for your interests. These "For Sale By Owner" sellers are called FSBO (pronounced "fizz-bow") in the industry, and sellers will sometimes take this route in an attempt to save money—usually theirs.

They may be pricing the home at what they think is the full market value and intending to pocket the difference. However, their pricing may be way high or way low, and they may also lack the expertise to make sure the sale documents meet all applicable regulations and give you a clear title. While you would not want to dismiss a FSBO home out of hand, you may want to hire your own buyer's agent as described later in this chapter to protect your interests.

What's In A Name?

Before you choose an agent, you need to understand both the different titles real estate practitioners use and the types of agency relationships you can have with them.

AGENT—An agent is licensed by a state real estate commission to assist in the buying, selling, leasing, and exchanging of real property. This person works under the direction of a real estate broker.

BROKER—A broker is licensed by a real estate commission to act independently to conduct a real estate brokerage business. In most states, that person must have one or more years experience as an agent and pass an extra examination.

REALTOR—A Realtor is a licensed real estate broker who is a member of the National Association of Realtors and subscribes to its

Code of Ethics. A Realtor may be working independently or with another Realtor. Licensed agents or brokers who are working in the office of a current Realtor may belong to the National Association of Realtors as REALTOR ASSOCIATES. Not everyone who is a licensed agent or broker is also a Realtor (and real Realtors are very proud of their professional designation and are offended when it is applied to a non-member).

Kinds of Representation

There are three basic ways, called "agency," that your agent can represent you in a real estate transaction. Early in your relationship, you need to decide which type of agency will work best for you, and you may be asked to sign an agency disclosure form to solidify the relationship. When you consider your choice, you should be aware that the agency relationship is not restricted to the agent you are dealing with. It actually refers to the broker who is responsible for the work done by the agents in the office where your agent works.

The Seller's Broker (or listing broker) is the traditional real estate representative used by buyers although few have realized it. The Seller's Broker's job has been to find a buyer for the listing. Unless you have hired a Buyer's Broker, any agent who shows the seller's listing, is technically a sub-agent of the listing broker and owes a fiduciary responsibility to the seller. This situation results from the fact that the listing broker has probably placed his listing with a Multiple Listing Service (MLS) where, according to the agreement your agent signed to belong to the service, he becomes a sub-agent to the listing broker and shares in his commission.

So if you tell "your" agent something that would materially affect the seller's response to your offer, he has a responsibility to give that information to the seller's agent or broker. In addition, if your agent learns something that would benefit you to the detriment of the seller, it would be unethical for your agent to give you that information.

Obviously there can be problems with this kind of arrangement. Your agent may be the best and most knowledgeable person you have, as a single, to confide in and hash things out with during the sales process. You have every right to expect that your agent will have your best interests at heart. To get that kind of service, you need a Buyer's Broker.

By choosing a Buyer's Broker, you are stating that you want your agent (who may be the broker or an agent working under the supervision of the broker) to work only on your behalf. The mode of payment here becomes somewhat negotiable. Sometimes it can still be paid as half the selling agent's commission by including that condition in the offer to buy. Other times you may have agreed to pay the buyer's agent's share of the commission or you may have hired your agent on an hourly basis or for a flat fee. The two of you will need to work this out at the beginning of your working relationship.

Keeping Your Priorities Clear

Randy Welch in Denver advises others to be sure they keep their priorities clear when they are dealing with an agent. As a single buyer, Welch trusted his friend, a real estate agent, to protect his interests.

On one hand, Welch's friend (who became his agent) lived in the building that he suggested Welch buy into. The friend was on the homeowners association's board of directors, so he knew how fiscally sound the association was. On the other hand, the friend was also the listing agent for a seller who was moving and had listed his unit below the original purchase price because of declining market values in the area.

This is where Welch feels he may have shortchanged himself. His agent/friend explained that his fiduciary responsibility in this transaction was to the seller, and Welch decided to ignore that speech since he felt emotionally that his friend would primarily look out for his interests. Wrong.

As his friend had explained, his fiduciary responsibility was to the seller in this transaction, but he was willing to act as a dual agent, serving both parties. Welch decided to make his offer on the unit based on the financial evaluation of his friend and agent. Once the offer was quickly accepted, it occurred to Welch that if he had hired a Buyer's Broker, he may have been advised to make a lower initial offer, and he may have been able to buy the unit for less money.

How do things stand now? Welch is a little sheepish that he may not have gotten the best deal possible. At the same time, he acknowledges that the responsibility for that rests squarely with him. As Welch's friend, his agent was able to find a unit that uniquely suited Welch's personal and professional needs (Welch is a writer and his unit at the end of a court provides the quiet he craves).

Still, Welch has some niggling regrets about not being as savvy a consumer as he wishes he had been. On the other hand, he agrees that his agent fulfilled his job competently and ethically, because his agent had neither the incentive nor the obligation to advise Welch to make a lower offer.

Fortunately, the upshot is that Welch was able to buy the unit he wanted, and he and his agent are still friends. However, if you want to avoid the problems Welch faced, be sure you understand the agency relationship you have with your agent.

When An Agent Serves Two Masters

In the event you are interested in buying a home that was listed through the same broker your agent is using, you have two choices. You can either accept Dual Agency or find a new agent.

If Dual Agency is contemplated, that fact should be made very clear to both parties and should preferably be agreed to in writing. Since this means that the same broker will be overseeing the seller's contracts and yours, there is an inherent possibility of conflict of interest. If you are uncomfortable working this way, it can be best just to change agents.

At this time, 44 states and the District of Columbia have legislation or regulations mandating agency disclosure. This means that if the agent you are talking to is contractually bound to act on behalf of another party in the transaction, the agent must inform you of that fact in writing. The states where you do not necessarily have the benefit of agency disclosure are Arizona, Arkansas, Kentucky, New Jersey, North Carolina, and Oregon.

Changes Are Coming

Now that you understand all of that, be prepared to have it all change. The tradition of having the agent who found a buyer for a property work as a sub-agent to the seller's agent became common practice as the Multiple Listing Service gained popularity according to Sharon Millett, chair of the National Association of Realtors Presidential Advisory Group on Agency. Before that, agents in the office that listed the property usually also found a buyer.

However, with the advent of the MLS, brokers from different offices were working together on home sales and they wanted to clarify where their fiduciary responsibilities lay. Millett says that the policy which was developed by the Association automatically obligated Realtors to represent the sellers in real estate transactions even if they were the agent who found the buyer.

Recognizing the changing marketplace and the fact that many agents are already working as Buyer's Brokers, the Presidential Advisory Group on Agency recommended making sub-agency optional (rather than mandatory as it traditionally has been). The hope was that this would clear up potential ethics concerns voiced by Realtors who chose to work as Buyer's Brokers.

The Association agreed to make sub-agency an option and this became effective in July of 1993. However, as a consumer, you still need to clarify whether your agent will be functioning as a sub-agent of the seller or as a Buyer's Broker. If you have a strong preference for the protection of a Buyer's Broker, be sure the agent you choose is experienced in working that way.

How To Choose An Agent

The real estate agent you choose will determine how smoothly your home buying experience goes. One way to find an agent you will like working with is to ask your friends about the agents who have helped them.

If you are asking friends, co-workers, or people in your church or social group for recommendations, be sure to ask them about the strengths and weaknesses of the agent they recommend. Were all their questions answered? Were their problems handled quickly, efficiently, and professionally?

Sometimes, you may not be able to get referrals you are comfortable with from friends, family, or co-workers. If not, there are several options you can pursue. One is to call your local Association of Realtors. Ask for the names of the top three or four officers of their organization. Then call those officers (who are often among the most successful local brokers), and ask them to refer you to the agent in their office who is most experienced in working with unmarried and/or first-time buyers.

Some people favor looking through the neighborhood they think they may want to move into and interviewing the agents who have the most For Sale signs out with their names on them. The potential problem with this is that some agents specialize in getting listings and representing sellers. They may not work frequently with buyers.

Another way to find a buyer's agent is to contact local real estate firms that have a relocation department. The relocation specialists can refer you to agents through their office who specialize in working with buyers (often buyers who are facing special challenges).

What To Look For

There are two things you may find especially helpful to consider in the initial stages of finding your agent. First, if you have not bought a home before—or lately—look for someone who specializes in working with first-time buyers. They will be more likely to be helpful with all your questions. Second, look for someone who either is single or who regularly works with single buyers. Another agent may sympathize with the unique challenges you face, but you may be better served by someone whose lifestyle or experience gives them more personal insight into your situation.

Also, if you are interested in moving into a particular area, look for agents who are familiar with that neighborhood or development. While any agent can check into the normal concerns like school quality or comparable sales, someone who is personally involved in the community is more likely to be aware of potential problems like whether the homes are downwind of a sewage treatment plant or come under an airport approach pattern during certain times.

Risky Business

You might also visit homes that are being shown as "open houses" in the neighborhoods you are interested in living. The agent who is sitting in the home may work for the listing broker and/or may be interested in working with single buyers.

But not always. Sometimes the listing agent will decide to do something else that day, and he may get someone else from his office to sit in the house and show it to people who come by. Unfortunately, the people who are most likely to be available for sitting in open homes may frequently be the people who have the least going on in their own professional lives. So be careful to ask about the qualifications of the agent if you visit an open house and are interested in the property or are looking for a local agent who can help you.

Also, if you cold-call a real estate office, you will get the person who has been assigned to work the phones and/or front desk. Again, this person is likely be someone who has time to spare. If you must cold-call, consider asking the person who answers the phone for the broker. When you reach her, ask her for the agent in her office who most closely meets your personal needs.

Now, a recommendation that may bother some people. Ask the agent you are talking to if he or she is a full-time agent. While it is possible to teach school, photograph weddings, or sell insurance, and still function as a real estate agent, the increasing sophistication required in real estate transactions makes it difficult for anyone to competently serve the needs of their client if they consider real estate a part-time job. They may not be able to keep as up-to-date on the quick-changing regulations and financing market or even the daily updates on new listings that may meet your needs. Also, his or her limited availability may lead to delays in your ability to close the sale.

Remember, a home is the largest investment most people will ever make. If you would not trust your life to a part-time doctor or your investment portfolio to an advisor who spends his days design-ing furniture, then it makes a certain amount of sense to confine your search for a real estate advisor to someone who specializes in home buyers.

The Rule Of Three

Now a caveat. You should interview at least three agents before you pick one. This is not a beauty contest. You are looking for the person who best meshes with your personality and who best appears to be able to handle the complicated transactions necessary to complete a home sale. He or she must also be aware of the special needs you face as a single. Beware of people who promise you the moon. They may actually be lost in space somewhere between fantasy and reality.

As you interview the agents, there are certain questions you should ask. Compare their answers among the agents you interview, and remember to ask each agent for three references of buyers (preferably single) they have worked with lately. Then be sure to check the references the agents offer, and ask them about their experiences with the agent, and how they wish it had been different.

Questions To Ask Potential Real Estate Agents

As a single, first-time buyer, interviewing prospective agents can be difficult. Here are some questions you can ask to help you get a feel for which agent you may best work with.

1. Are you a licensed broker or agent? (If they say "agent" then verify their employment with their broker.)
2. Are you a Realtor?
3. How long have you been working in this field?
4. Do you do this full-time?
5. How many sales have you closed in the last 6 months?
6. Have you earned any professional designations? If so, which ones? *
7. How long have you worked this neighborhood/community?
8. Can you give me the names of three recent clients as references?

---

* Earning special designations like Certified Residential Specialist (C.R.S.) and Certified Real Estate Broker (C.R.B.) tends to show that the agent is especially interested in being the best professional she can be.

9. How do you plan to find me a home?
10. What kind of help do you expect from me?
11. How often will I receive progress reports from you?
12. What kind of assistance can you give me with getting pre-qualified for financing?

Three No-No's

While you have authorized someone to act as your agent, that does not mean they can do anything they want and do it in your name. Three major no-no's are:

1. FAILURE TO DISCLOSE: All agents are required to report defective or adverse conditions in a property you are considering if those conditions could reasonably be discovered by you, an inspector, or another agent. In some states, the seller must sign a disclosure statement attesting to the condition of the property.

2. REFUSE TO PRESENT OFFERS: Your agent must present any legitimate offers you make to the seller's agent even if your agent does not feel your offer is adequate and even if the seller has already accepted an offer from someone else.

3. ACT WITHOUT YOUR APPROVAL: Normally, your agent must present all offers to the seller's agent in a timely manner. Your agent must have your approval to accept or reject any counteroffers made by the seller.

What You Can Expect

Perhaps the most important skill a good agent has is the ability to listen. While you happen to be single, that does not mean your needs are cookie-cutter predictable. Your lifestyle is unique to you, and you deserve an agent who is not stuck in some media-inspired vision of what your lifestyle must be.

The agents you interview should also be asking you questions. Where do you work? How and how long do you prefer to commute? Do you need schools nearby? What social activities are important to you? Do you want the responsibility of yard work?

If you have completed the Lifestyle Choices Worksheet in Chapter 1, you may want to bring it out and discuss it with the agents you are interviewing to help them understand your goals.

How Much Competition Is Healthy?

Sometimes people feel that they will get the best results by getting several agents to compete against each other for the opportunity to find them a house. However, this may offend the better agents. If your agent is acting as a buyer's agent, she may feel that it could take a certain amount of time to help you identify the exact qualities you want in a home and work out your financing options.

If she goes to check out a potential property on the MLS and discovers that three other agents are doing the same thing for you, then all of the agents are likely to lose interest in working with you. So pick an agent and work with her. If after a reasonable period, you feel that your needs are not being adequately addressed, it may be time to have a serious talk with your agent (and possibly your agent's broker), or move on to someone new.

Where Does The Commission Go?

A brief note about the commission. It can be tempting to see the commission figures on the closing documents and feel like real estate must be the easiest way ever invented to make money. In reality, agents can make a good living, but it may be harder than you think.

For instance, if a home sells for $100,000 and the commission is 6 percent, then the amount of commission paid is $6,000. However, even a traditional equal split between the seller's agent and your agent (assuming you did not use a Buyer's Broker and negotiate a separate fee), would mean that each party got $3,000. Now, each agent will normally have to split his $3,000 with his broker to pay for the supervision and support services the agent receives through the office. While that split is negotiated by the parties and will depend on a number of factors including the amount of support given the agent and the agent's track record, we will assume the split is 50/50 and the agent is now down to $1,500. Then, after taxes and other business expenses like car upkeep, you may decide that the hourly rate your agent makes on your deal is not quite as attractive as you first thought.

If you are reading this and saying to yourself that you do not need an agent, you can handle your deal yourself, good luck. If you have the time to search out available homes (probably without the Multiple Listing Service since it is only available to members), the expertise to know all the applicable laws and regulations, the time to check with a variety of lenders and compare their rates and qualification standards, and the ability to negotiate your position dispassionately, you should be successful.

However, for the same reasons that most people choose to hire a mechanic to fix their carburetor or a physician to remove their appendix, most buyers choose to hire a real estate agent. There is no substitute for experience.

7

Something New— Or—Tried And True?

Something New

There is nothing quite like the feeling of walking into a brand new home and knowing it is yours. Everything is fresh, new, and clean— and you don't have to start by un-doing someone else's personal touches.

Most people who buy a new home will choose one in a tract or a spec home being built by a local builder. A new home is a wonderful thing, but it comes with its own set of joys and challenges.

Choosing A New Home

It can be easier than you think to fall in love with a model home. As you walk through, you can just imagine yourself living there, enjoying that cozy kitchen, relaxing with friends in the living room— and maybe enjoying a whirlpool bath after a hard day at work.

There is a reason people in the industry sometimes refer to the group of model homes surrounded by a fence as a "trap." It is nothing nefarious, it is just that once you begin looking at the homes, the only way back out is usually through the sales office.

When you are looking at new homes, take along a copy of your Lifestyle Choices Worksheets and the list below to help you keep your mind on your own goals. Remember, the homes you are looking at have probably been decorated by professionals. Everything from the music playing in the background, to the flowers, the children's books open in the small bedroom, and even the kitchen table set for breakfast, are all designed to touch your heart and convince you to buy. These things can make it very difficult to really see the house as it would be if you buy (unless, of course, you manage to buy the model home—furnished!).

The builder may have brochures of the development you can take with you. If so, make notes on the sheets showing the floor plans you like.

You may want to keep a tape measure in your pocket and quickly measure any important rooms where you might be considering keeping special, oversized furniture, like a pool table. Also, if you are planning to use a small bedroom for a home office, you will need to be sure your desk, bookshelves, files and other furniture will fit comfortably (in models, they tend to show a home office with little more than a modest sized desk in it so the room will look bigger).

If you do think you like a particular home, do stop by the sales office on the way out for more information. Now is a good time to ask a few questions:

1. Who is the builder, and what else has he or she built locally?
2. Does the builder offer special financing? Often, builders can arrange below-market-rate loans because of the large value of mortgages that will be written in a tract.
3. Can you prequalify me for the financing you offer?
4. Exactly what is covered in the price? Many of the things you loved may be "decorator" items. The built-in bookshelves, the fancy window treatments, and wallpaper may not even be available through the builder at all. Other things like ceramic tile countertops, mirrored closet doors, extra-thick carpeting, and intercom systems may only be available at an extra cost.
5. Are there any special assessments that I will have to pay? Special fees for building streets, putting in lighting, or installing and

maintaining landscaping can add a nasty and unexpected shock to your payments.

6. Can you give me a price list for the upgrades? While the prices may change on some items while you are making your decision, the builder's agents should be able to give you a good idea of what your choices will be and what they may cost on everything from upgraded appliances and carpets to fencing and landscaping.

7. Can you have a blank copy of the purchase contract? You should read this and show it to your Buyer's Broker and/or your attorney. They can tell you about any problems you may face down the line. One might be that the builder will not guarantee the price until the home is ready to move into. That could mean that you could face a dramatic rise in price at the last minute, possibly making the home too expensive for you to afford.

Check Out The Builder

Once you have gone home, check out the builder. First, do look at other neighborhoods built by the same developer and talk to people there. If you were able to get references from the builder, check them out too—but remember that the builder expected these people to say nice things.

Check with the state licensing body and the Better Business Bureau for problems. A friendly call to the local union hiring halls might elicit some candid comments about the quality of the builder's work and reputation. You might also call the city planning department to see if there are any problems with the builder or this tract. This may seem tedious, but buying a home is a major purchase, and you want to be sure you get what you pay for.

As described in Chapter 5, you may want to have a Buyer's Broker to help you look at the house and advise you. Remember, those friendly sales agents at the office in the development work for the builder, not you. In addition to counseling you on the sale, the agent may also be able to help you decide which upgrades are likely to pay for themselves at resale in the local marketplace.

Once you are ready to sign a contract, be sure to add two more items that are not likely to already appear in it.

First, make your purchase depend on your receiving an acceptable report from a home inspector of your choice. This will enable you to be as sure as possible that the home you are buying is built competently. If, for instance, your inspector discovers that the insulation is not as promised or the grading encourages rain to puddle next to the foundation, you can insist these problems be fixed or the contract is off. The builder may tell you that all those kinds of problems will be caught on the final "walk-through" you do with their representative so you do not really need to hire an inspector. That works best where the builder is interested in buyer satisfaction. Not all are. So, unless you are a professional inspector, you could miss out on identifying some very expensive things that will need fixing later. The money you spend on a professional inspection will be well spent.

Second, you want a Home Owners Warranty policy, backed by the builder and an insurance company. The facts of life today are that even some excellent builders will go out of business for various reasons. And some builders will incorporate under different names for each subdivision to reduce their legal exposure if major problems should arise later. If serious problems with the structure or operating systems do come up within the prescribed time frame, you would normally try to get the builder to fix them. Failing that, the Home Owners Warranty policy will pay for the repairs. Many times, builders will pay for this policy because of the protection it also offers them.

On The Other Hand

Unfortunately, in a really hot market, all bets are off. Newspapers have carried stories about new home developments in very desirable areas where people have camped out front for days just for a chance to bid on a home.

When this happens, there is no time to take the paperwork home and consider it. The builder will probably be working on a take-it-or-leave-it basis. After all, there are plenty of people in line behind you.

Your best defense here is to be prepared before you start. As soon as you decide you are going to look at new homes, start asking around about different builders who work regularly in your area. Check them out in the different ways described earlier in this chapter.

Then, contact the builders who check out as good bets, and ask their sales or public relations department about upcoming projects. Sometimes you may be able to get your name on a priority list even before the homes are made available for sale. At the very least, you should be able to find out when and where new offerings will be made.

Minor Inconveniences

Keep in mind that there can be some inconveniences in buying a new home. If you are buying in a tract development at the edge of town, you may find that some simple services like cable TV and daily newspaper delivery will not be available to you right away. More important inconveniences could include not having public transportation out that far yet, and if you have a child, that child may have to be bussed long distances to school if there is not already one in the neighborhood.

You may also want to watch your budget carefully when you are picking extras and upgrades that will be included in the sales price. The added dollars may not seem like much if you are planning to sell this home in a few years and move up to something nicer. But if you are planning to stay for a long time, ask yourself if you really want to be paying interest on those drapes and carpets for 30 years—long after they may have worn out and been replaced. You may find it much more economical to wait for some things and charge others on your regular charge cards and pay them off quickly.

At the end of this chapter is a checklist to help you as you look at newly constructed homes. Photocopy it, and use a fresh sheet for each home you are considering.

Yvonne Costello chose to buy a newly constructed home for many reasons. A major one, she says, was that new homes tend to appreciate in value more quickly than resale. Her assumption was right here. After only four years, her home in Camarillo, California, is worth one and a half times what she paid for it.

But more than the money, she wanted a new home because it would allow her to express her individuality through her choices of colors and materials without having to remove someone else's choices first. Even the landscaping came into the equation because she wanted a beautiful combination of fruit trees and custom brick walks. "Designing the landscaping was something I could create and do," she states happily. "I chose exactly what I wanted."

Tried And True

Buying a resale home can be an excellent choice for a single. Unlike a new home, it will come complete with landscaping, drapes, and other expensive incidentals already in place. You are moving into an established neighborhood where the social customs (not to mention the trees) have deep roots.

There are going to be a number of considerations you need to keep in mind if you are looking at resale housing. Mindbender: Have you ever noticed that it is "used" cars but "resale" housing? Probably because "used" cars rarely appreciate in value. On the other hand, used homes usually do.

Here Comes The Judge

When it comes to choosing a home, you are the best judge of what will satisfy your needs. You should use your Lifestyle Choices Worksheet in Chapter 1 to help you determine what you need and want. Referring back to it frequently can seem silly, but by doing that you are reinforcing your choices in your mind. Then, if a perfectly spectacular home becomes available in your price range, but does not have space for the home office you really have to have, you can reject it before you fall in love with it.

Your Agent's Job

Once you have chosen an agent, she will be working closely with you through the process. You will want to have a regular schedule of contacts both to remind your agent of your continuing interest and to answer any questions you may have. For instance, you are undoubtedly talking about your home buying plans with friends, family, and co-workers. Sometimes these people may pass on myths and mistaken information they have picked up through the years. So before you accept what they say as gospel, talk about it with your agent.

Comparing Apples With . . .

Once your agent has helped you prequalify for financing, you are ready to look at homes. Assuming your agent is an MLS member (and most agents are), he will search through the local Multiple Listing Service to find homes in your price range that may suit your needs. He will then arrange for you to visit the homes that interest you.

You do not want to go empty handed. Photocopy your Lifestyle Choices Worksheets in Chapter 1 to take with you. Also make blank copies of the chart at the end of this chapter so you will have a fresh form for each home you visit. Keeping records of each interesting home you consider can help refresh your memory later on after you have seen several homes. Too often, the individual amenities can become confused in your memory after you have seen a few homes.

You might also like to bring an instant camera along. Use it to take a photo of the front of the house to go with your worksheet and take other shots to help you record any unique features of the home. If you have any large special items like a grand piano or an heirloom dining room table you want to bring to your new home, you should bring a tape measure along to ensure you will be able to fit them in any home you are seriously considering.

Keep an eye out for fliers when you visit different homes. Many times the seller's agent will prepare a simple flier or brochure about the house. It might include information about the size and number of rooms, amenities like fireplaces and hardwood floors, and financial information including the asking price and special details like the assumability of the mortgage. This, along with your own notes will be helpful when you are considering the relative merits of different homes.

Your agent can be especially helpful in helping you notice things in each house that you should consider. She may point out that you might want to put a contingency clause for inspecting an older roof or other items that may require special attention.

Shopping In The Sunshine

Be sure you visit any home you are considering during daylight hours so you can get an accurate picture of how it looks inside and out. You might also make it a point to drive by the home later at different times of the day or days of the week.

Ideally, you may see people out jogging, walking their dogs, and talking with each other. On the other hand, you may discover that the street in front of the home is the weekend gathering place for noisy young adults or that commuters whiz past twice a day using the street as a short cut.

Your agent can also help you become familiar with the neighborhoods where the homes you are considering are located. He can get you information about property taxes, school quality, city services, transportation, social activities, entertainment opportunities, and many agents will even help you get information about crime statistics for the area.

Don't be discouraged if you don't find your dream home in the first few weeks. The right home for you may come on the market any day, and a good agent will keep working on your behalf until he finds it.

You can tell your friends, family, and co-workers that you are looking for a home and basically what you are hoping to find. From time to time, everyone hears of someone who is about to offer their home for sale. By keeping an ear out for these opportunities, you may be able to make an offer on a property that suits you before anyone else learns about it.

Penny Wise, Pound Foolish

On occasion, you may be viewing an attractive home when the owner pulls you aside and offers to sell the home to you at a discount if you will help them cut the agents out of the picture. In reality, what you are setting yourself up for is a lot of hassle and heartache if you try this route.

If the seller has an agent, the contract between them probably states that if their work during the contract brings in a buyer—even if that buyer does not make an offer for months afterwards—the agent is entitled to a commission. And you can believe that any agent who is released will continue to follow the sale record on that home for that period. In the event that you have signed a Buyer's Broker agreement with your agent and have been able to negotiate a payment to that agent based on the sale price of the home, you may still owe your agent his fee.

Even more discouraging is the fact that if you decide to wait out the period the seller would owe his agent a commission after that agreement has expired, you may find that someone else has come in during your wait and made a successful offer on the home or the seller has changed his mind and will not be selling after all.

For the first-time buyer, the portion of the price you end up paying for the home that ends up supporting the agents' commissions may be more than offset by the value of the help you receive in negotiating the sale and finding advantageous financing.

Also, don't discount the value of other counsel your agent may give you. If your agent tells you the home you are considering is on a flood plain, it may change your opinion about buying it. Without that advice, you may have bought a home that would be under water after the next big storm.

The Seduction Of Curb Appeal

Every seller has been told by their agent that "curb appeal" is going to help sell their home. Normally, the seller will do as much as they feel is necessary to make their home attractive to prospective buyers. If they have a savvy agent, they have also been counseled on "staging" their home inside. The goal here is to give it the appeal of a new model home.

When the seller has done his homework, the avocado green flocked wallpaper is long gone. The collection of 400 sets of salt and pepper shakers the seller normally has on display are packed up, out of sight. In fact, some sellers will rent a mini-storage unit and move a lot of their furniture and decorator items there to make the home appear larger. They may even have rented new furniture to freshen the home's appearance.

While this can help keep you from being distracted from the house by its contents, you will need to stay aware of the way scale can be used to fool the eye. A living room that looks charming when furnished with only a love seat, chair, and small coffee table will look entirely different after you try to fit your full-sized couch and recliner into it.

At other homes, the seller may not have done anything to "stage" his home. Here is where you need to practice self control and use your artistic eye. You will have to ignore the plaid couch in front of the flowered drapes and the bright orange carpeting. Try to see the home as a series of spaces, and decide if those spaces meet your living needs. If that is difficult, you may want to sketch the layout of the house (and maybe measure it with a tape measure or by pacing it off). That may help you evaluate the property better.

The good news for bargain hunters is that all things considered, a house that is beautifully "staged" will sell for more than the same house with hideous decorating. While you may incur some extra expenses for redecorating the hideous home, you can control the timing and amount of those expenses and you may save a good deal of money overall.

Splendor In The Grass

When you are looking at a house, be sure to get a good look at the yard around it. There can be a big difference in the amount of time and effort it takes to keep up two yards of the same size. Elaborate plantings and large beds of annuals are beautiful, but they will take more time than caring for grass with a few trees.

Especially if you will be living there alone, you might want to ask the seller how much time he normally spends on yard work every week or month. Does that meet with the time you expect to have available? If not, will you be able to hire a gardener to help you?

Buyer Beware

When you are buying a resale condominium, there is something you need to be careful about.

Condominiums offer a relatively care-free lifestyle—if you are careful which one you choose. Some condos were originally apartments that were converted to condos. On occasion, the conversion may have been primarily cosmetic with new paint and a redecorated lobby. So if the condo is new but the building is actually old, you can be buying a home with heating, plumbing, and other systems that may need major repairs or replacements soon. This could result in new assessments for you within a few years of moving in unless there is an adequate reserve fund to pay for it.

If you are considering purchasing a resale condominium (or any resale home that is subject to a homeowners association), you should ask the association if there have been any problems with the unit that you might not be aware of like unapproved changes to the unit or unpaid assessments.

Look Before You Leap (Home Inspections)

It can be especially important to insist on getting the home inspected if it is a resale. According to the American Society of Home Inspectors, approximately half of the resale homes on the market have at least one significant defect and virtually all of them need some maintenance and repair work.

The number one problem is improper grading and drainage around the house which can lead to water sitting against the house. The second most frequently found problem area is the electrical system, including amateurish and often dangerous wiring connections. Other major problems with homes that were inspected include roof damage and mechanical problems with the heating and air conditioning systems.

If you are not familiar with ways to maintain a home, the inspection report will give you tips about things you should keep an eye on. It will note whether you need to trim trees and large shrubs which may overhang the house, scraping the roof, and clogging the gutters with droppings.

It will also note places where you may need to replace bathroom caulk or grout; this is necessary not just to improve the appearance. Leaks can allow water to seep down and lead to hidden rot—which will be a lot more expensive to repair than the original grout repair would have been. Your report should also point out any potential safety hazards at the home like flammable products being stored near heaters, water heaters, and fireplaces.

Older homes have special problems not often seen in new homes. Plumbing changes and updates over the years may have resulted in having incompatible metals joining each other—and corroding each other out. Sometimes renovations in the home have been done without considering what walls were supporting the house and roof. If sagging is occurring, a consultation with a professional engineer may be required.

Another common problem with older homes is a lack of energy efficiency in everything from uninsulated walls and ceilings to loose, drafty windows.

Once you have made an offer on a house and included a contingency clause calling for a home inspection, the next thing you need to do is find an inspector. Here, your real estate agent may be able to help if she has worked with local inspectors in the past.

Unfortunately, Texas is the only state that makes any effort to license home inspectors as of this writing and there is no nationally recognized credential inspectors can earn to show their professionalism.

What they *can* do is apply for membership in the American Society of Home Inspectors, Inc. (ASHI). ASHI members are independent professionals who have met rigorous professional and education requirements and who pledge to a strict code of ethics. One of the ethical standards they are adamant about is that the inspector not use the inspection as a way of generating work doing repairs.

If you want referral to ASHI members in your area, you can call (708) 290-1919. For more detailed information about what is, or is not, included in a home inspection, ask for a copy of ASHI's Standards of Practice brochure.

In the end, the home you are considering does not pass or fail the inspection. You are just given detailed information that can assist you in making a decision about whether to complete the transaction.

If your agent helped you write your contingency clause correctly, it should give you the right to get out of the transaction (and get your deposit back) if you do not get a "satisfactory" inspection report. However, if there are problems, you do not necessarily have to walk away from the deal. If there is significant negative information in the report, you may want to use it to negotiate with the seller for either a lower purchase price or seller-paid repairs.

Should You Get A Warranty Policy?

Diane Rooney of Lakewood, Ohio, swears she will never buy another house unless it has a home warranty. While her new home is a beautiful setting for her contemporary art collection it has not come without problems.

In early 1991 she moved into a home she admits she bought as an impulse purchase although she had looked at a lot of homes over time. (In fact, a single, she admits to storming out of a few of them when the agents who were showing them asked her if she wanted to check with her husband before she made any decisions.)

She had the house inspected, but it was done on a snowy day in December, and the report contained a lot of disclaimers, such as saying the drains ran slow. After getting a basement full of water and a $2,000 bill from a plumber to snake out and repair the pipes, Rooney discovered that the three beautiful oak trees in her yard were sending roots into the pipe system. Now she cautions other singles to *always* get a warranty. It would have saved her a lot of money on plumbing and other repairs.

What does a home warranty cover? When you, the builder or seller purchase a Home Buyer's Warranty for your new or resale home, you get several kinds of coverage. First, you get coverage for structural defects (the length of the coverage depends in part on the age of the home). Second, you can get coverage for the major systems in your home. So if the hot water heater stops getting hot during the policy period, it will be replaced. For new homes, you can even get one year of protection on workmanship and materials (for instance, rust on your railings).

Home Choice Checklist

Photocopy this checklist and take copies of it whenever you are looking at a home you might buy. Keep it together with any brochures, photos or other information you get on a particular home so you can refer to it later when you are making your decisions.

Address

Contact (agent, developer, etc.)_____

Phone (___)_____

Exterior finish (brick, wood, etc.)   _____

Price   _____

Financing Available   _____
      (i.e., FHA, VA, Bond Program,
      or assumable mortgage on resale)   _____

FEATURES	Excellent	Average	Poor
Investment value			
Access to transportation			
Access to cultural activities			
Access to shopping			
Close to schools			
Privacy			
Safety/security			
Exterior landscaping			
Fences			
Basement/Attic			
Energy Efficiency			
Wall insulation			
Ceiling insulation			
Double-pane windows			
Bedrooms—Number/Size			
Bathrooms—Number/Size			
Living Room			
Dining Room			
Kitchen			
Family Room			
Views			
Light			
Architectural Interest			
(high ceilings, pot			
shelves, etc.)			

Fireplaces
Appliances—gas/electric
    Oven/stove
    Refrigerator
    Dishwasher
Other Miscellaneous

    _____
    _____
    _____

8

Have I Got A
Deal For You

Once you find a home you like and can afford, it is time to make an offer. The key here is to remember that while you want the sellers to accept the deal you are offering, you are not out to make them like you. Real estate professionals refer to a contract as a "meeting of the minds," not a sealing of a friendship.

In a sense you and the sellers are adversaries. Their goal is to realize the highest price possible for their home. Your goal is to get the home at the best possible price with whatever other concessions you want (like having them leave the refrigerator).

Review Your Strategy

This is also a good time to mentally review your relationship with your agent or the developer's salesperson. Unless you have hired a buyer's agent as described in Chapter 6, your agent's fiduciary responsibility is as a sub-agent of the seller's agent. That means that if you make an offer, but tell your agent you would be willing to go up $5,000, your agent is duty bound to tell the seller's agent that fact.

In terms of negotiating, only a Buyer's Broker can actually negotiate price, conditions or other terms solely on your behalf. If you ask your traditional agent if the seller is likely to take $15,000 less, all this agent can do is reiterate the terms in the original offer to sell. However, he may share some information about the seller's needs that the seller is comfortable having him share such as her need to stay in the home until a certain date. Anything more would require he get the seller's consent before giving you the information.

Married people often use each other as a sounding board and confidante during negotiations. They may even develop a negotiating strategy like the traditional "good cop/bad cop" mode. As a single, if you really need someone to support and counsel you through the negotiation process, you should be sure that person has your best interests at heart. Either hire a buyer's agent or an attorney to advise and possibly represent you.

Win-Win Negotiations

By planning ahead, you can create a situation where you and the seller both come out feeling like winners.

Before you even think about making an offer, see how much you can find out about the seller. Is he in a hurry to sell because of financial hardship or a pending closing on his next home? (Subtext: Is he likely to accept a low-ball offer?) Does she need to take out all her equity or would it be possible for her to take back a second mortgage from you for part of the sale price? Do the sellers have special needs—like moving when school is out—that you might be able to offer to deal with, making your offer more attractive?

You also need to get a feeling for the real market value of the home. Your agent should be able to get you "comps" (data on what similar homes have sold for recently). Be sure you are comparing apples with apples. If one of the homes has a pool, fireplace, extra bedrooms or other valuable features that the other home does not, you need to allow for that when you determine a fair value for the home you are bidding on.

If your agent can not give you satisfactory comps, you may want to hire an independent appraiser to evaluate the property. After all, a few hundred dollars for an expert opinion may save you thousands in the offer you make to the seller. The only drawback here is that in a very hot seller's market, you may not be able to schedule an appraisal before someone else makes a successful offer for the home. However, if you have already talked to lenders, you may be able to use an appraiser approved by the lender you are considering using. Having an appraisal already done by someone they use could speed up your loan approval if you decide on this property. In that case, be sure to structure the appraisal contract so you do not end up paying twice for the same work—once directly and again through the lender.

Finally, you need a negotiating plan. Since you have already evaluated the seller's needs as you have been able to determine them, you should have thought about ways to integrate their needs with yours. Hint: Remember that the sellers are selling more than real estate, they are putting their memories on the line. It does not help to insult the current owner's taste in window treatments, and that ugly tree in the front yard may have been planted to memorialize a family event. Treat their space with the same respect you would want your own memories to receive if the situation were reversed.

Making Your Initial Offer

In a normal market, or one that favors buyers, you want to make your offer low enough to be attractive to you without insulting the seller (because that may prejudice them against you permanently). You also want to include some negotiating room for yourself. How much you offer in relation to the listed selling price is going to be determined by several factors. First, the state of the market. In a seller's market where houses are getting multiple offers within days (or even sometimes hours) of being listed, a low-ball offer will probably just be a waste of time.

When the seller's market is especially hot, sellers sometimes receive multiple offers that are all higher than the initial listing price and bidding wars have been known to happen. As a buyer, you may decide you have to give it your best shot first. Unfortunately, if it is not accepted, you have to be willing to stretch even further or walk away from the deal.

In a buyer's market where there are more homes for sale than buyers looking for them, you have more latitude. Depending on the local market conditions and the seller's degree of motivation, you may be able to strike a very good deal, well below the listing price. But, consider your own motivation. If this home meets all your requirements and fulfills all your hopes, do not antagonize the seller by making an offer way below the value of comparable sales. It will only make it harder to negotiate with this seller later in the process. On the other hand, if this is one of several acceptable properties you may want to take a chance at making a very low offer on the possibility that you may get lucky.

If you decide to make your first offer significantly below the listing price, you may encounter some resistance from your agent, especially if you have not hired a buyer's agent. Remember, that while the agent may honestly feel that the seller will not accept the offer, he also is motivated by the fact that the size of his paycheck is in direct relation to the size of the final selling price.

You should know that the seller's agent has to present every legitimate offer to the seller. That means an offer that is put in writing and includes a good-faith deposit. If your agent is not comfortable presenting your offer, and you feel the agent is pressuring you to please him, you may want to get a different agent. At the very least, you should consider talking to your agent's broker about the situation.

As in any negotiation, it is better to start from the low end and go up than start with your top offer and hope to come down. Be very clear in your own head about how high you are willing to go, and what you expect for that. Then stick to it. It can be better to walk away from a deal than buy a home you like, but that keeps you too broke to fix it up or even enjoy life.

As you are working up your negotiating plan, you might want to consider some areas where you might ask for or give concessions that are not strictly cash. For instance, you might want to consider asking the seller to include some appliances (which will lower the amount you need to spend right after closing), or ask the seller to pay part of your closing costs as part of your offer to reduce your end costs.

Contingencies—Your Safety Net

A contingency clause (sometimes called a condition clause) is a way to protect yourself against some problems you may not be aware of or able to assess yourself when you make your offer. It basically means that the deal is off unless certain conditions are met.

The kinds of contingencies you may include can cover the property, the financing, or even special considerations you need. Perhaps you need to close at a certain date to fulfill the requirements of your current lease. Maybe you want to close after a specified date to allow you to get your down payment out of a CD at its maturity so you do not have to pay a penalty.

Frequently buyers include a contingency clause that makes the sale subject to their ability to get adequate financing. You will want to be more specific than just "adequate." Otherwise, the seller can hold you to the bargain if you can qualify for any financing, no matter how unattractive the terms are to you.

In your contingency, you might specify that you want a 30-year fixed-rate mortgage with a rate of 10.5 percent and a total amount of $155,000.

Some mortgages can be assumed by the new buyer, but the lender normally has the right to approve or disapprove of the new buyer. If you are counting on assuming the current mortgage to enable you to buy the home, you will want a contingency clause for this situation. Also, if you are buying the home with a friend, you might also decide to include a clause specifying that he or she must be able to qualify for specific financing. To make this more palatable to the seller, you may give a time frame within which you will satisfy this contingency or the deal can be rescinded.

Be sure to allow yourself enough time. This is especially important during a busy market or at times like early 1992 when the financing pipeline was jammed by current homeowners trying to take advantage of low interest rates to refinance their homes.

You may also want to place contingencies that allow time for inspections you may want whether they are full inspections by a building inspector or specialized inspections of the roof, foundation, pool or plumbing. Your contingency should state that the inspections will be done within a certain time frame, and if the results are not satisfactory to you, the contract is void, and your deposit will be returned to you.

When Ace Rodin*, a graphic designer and sculptor in Lakewood, Colorado, included a clause that enabled him to cancel the contract if the inspection report was unacceptable, he never intended to have to use it. But later, he was sure glad it was there.

The house was older, built in 1926. It was also affordable. Rodin had even made a point of visiting the neighborhood at different times of the day to see what the street scene was like. So far, everything looked fine.

Then, the day the inspector came to the house, Rodin spent about four hours there with him. After watching a group of out-of-control

---

* Name changed to protect the person's privacy.

kids noisily horsing around and tearing the branches off the bushes out front, he finally understood why part of the fence gate was in the basement. He also noticed that the roofing trucks at the unkempt house next door were overflowing with bags of garbage. All this was giving him second thoughts about whether this home was for him.

Fortunately for him, the inspector found that the water main from the street was likely to fail in the next two years, resulting in thousands of dollars in repairs. On that basis, he backed out of the contract, saving himself from a home that promised a constant parade of expenses and irritation. Since then, Rodin purchased a townhouse at the end of a row of buildings, giving him the privacy and quiet he wanted in a home.

In addition, homeowners association regulations can inspire you to add contingency clauses. If the home you are making an offer on is subject to a homeowners association, you may want to include contingency clauses to the effect that your offer is subject to having your attorney or accountant approve the financial condition of the association.

This is also the time to include clauses about the deal being subject to receiving written confirmation from the association permitting any activities that might be important to you, like running a business or taking in a roommate, which appear to be restricted by the CC&R's.

Sometimes buyers also include a clause that makes the sale contingent on the approval of an attorney. The seller will most likely want to put a short time frame on this clause to keep you from using it as an all-purpose escape clause.

Do It In Writing

While this may seem to be one of those things that goes without saying, put your offer in writing. In some areas of the country, people sometimes will still make an offer verbally. This can be a BIG mistake since a verbal offer has no legal standing in the courts.

First, remember that childhood game where one person would whisper a story to the person next to her. The second child would pass it to the third, etc. By the time it got back to the original child, the story hardly ever was recognizable as the story she first started.

If you try to make an agreement verbally, you both are likely to have differing memories of exactly what you agreed on. Your deal also may not be enforceable if the seller gets and accepts a written offer he prefers before you two have formalized your deal.

Your agent will have form(s) you need to complete to make your formal offer. They will include the address or description of the property, the date, and your name—for starters.

If you are buying the home with a friend, you will want to be sure that you include a description with your name such as "John Johnson, a single man and Kim Clancy, a single woman." You will want to make it very clear so some typist along the way does not make your forms read as if you are married to each other. At the very least, it could postpone your closing if the forms are faulty. At worst, if it slides through and you sign the forms, it could make life more difficult when it comes time to sell.

The form will specify that the seller will deliver a marketable title to you, free and clear of encumbrances except those noted. It will state who will pay for the title insurance and the name of the title company.

There may be a listing of other expenses incurred during the sale, and you can say who you think should pay them. Your agent can be very helpful here. There will be some costs that are customarily paid by the seller in your area and others that are customarily paid by the buyer. The word here to remember is "customarily." Until the deal closes, everything is negotiable. If you have a small down payment, getting the seller to cover some of these costs normally paid by the buyer in your area can make it possible for you to close the deal.

The expenses that fall into this category can include (but are not limited to):

Escrow Fees
Title Search
Title Insurance
    Buyer
    Lender

Deed Preparation Fee
Recording Fee
Notary Fee
Documentary Transfer Taxes
City Transfer Taxes
County Transfer Taxes
Pest Control Inspection/Report
Inspection Fees
      Engineer
      Roof
      Pool
      Plumber
      Soils Engineer or Geologist
Home Warranty Policy

Making A Deposit

With your offer to buy, your agent will need to take a deposit. In most cases, if the seller signs the contract (and in some cases, accepts the deposit), the contract becomes binding.

The amount you decide to offer for a deposit is completely up to you. In some areas, it may be common to offer $1,000 as a deposit. In others, it may be five percent of the price offered. The seller wants as much as possible to show that you are earnest about buying the home. On the other hand, from your standpoint, it is best to offer as little as reasonable since if you decided to pull out, you could lose your deposit.

The time you might want to reconsider that would be in a hot seller's market. Some people feel that in a situation where two similar offers come in, the one with the largest deposit will win the day. However, others feel that you would be better to worry about submitting a clean, attractive offer with few contingencies that shows you are prequalified for financing if you want to impress the seller.

The Face Off

Now it is time to present your offer to the seller. Should you be there when it happens?

You do not have to actually be there. Your agent can present your offer for you. Unless he is a buyer's agent he can not unreservedly negotiate for you, but he can present your offer and bring back any acceptance or counteroffer the seller makes. Then you can also respond in writing. You can go back and forth like that until you come to an agreement or decide to back off.

If you do want someone to negotiate only for you, you can use your agent, or hire an attorney who is experienced in real estate negotiations to help. As a single, you may want to ask a friend who is a good negotiator to help even though your friend can not legally be paid for negotiating for you unless he is a real estate agent or an attorney. But to avoid any potential problems, it might be better to hire a professional to advise you.

When should you consider having someone negotiate for you? If you are prone to talking too much, especially when you are nervous, you may end up giving away more than you planned. It only takes a second to admit you might be willing to pay more—and, you can bet that the seller will want to make sure you do just that.

You may also find yourself waxing eloquent about the Christmas trees you plan to put in the bay window and the barbecues you are going to have on the patio. This kind of information lets the seller know you have your heart set on this home and may be convinced to pay more than you have already offered.

Finally, some people react to stressful situations by becoming blustery and overpowering. If your negotiating style is to try to bully people into agreeing with you, you may also find that you do better if you have someone else do your negotiating for you.

As a single, you can use your absence from the negotiations as a tool. For instance, if the seller is talking about making a counteroffer, your agent may suggest they offer to make certain concessions in exchange for other concessions from you. The seller's response can be to reject your agent's offer out of hand—or to express interest. If the seller is interested and writes a counteroffer to you, you know there is still some negotiating space left in the situation. At that time, you need to re-evaluate what you want from the negotiations and retailor your strategy accordingly.

Being There Is Half The Fun

If you get a kick out of going to garage sales and talking the sellers down in price, or negotiating the price of your new car, being there when your offer is presented can be a lot of fun. Just be sure you have decided what your bottom line will be before you begin—then stay with it.

Remember, you do not have to complete the negotiations at your first sitting. You may want to take their counteroffer home (or to your attorney) to consider it before you respond to anything you want more time to think about or research.

Your agent may discourage you from coming when he presents your offer. In part, he may be concerned that your inexperience will result in giving the seller more information that he can use in his negotiations. However, you may just be a better negotiator than your agent and save him from ruining your chances of getting the home. In any case, the decision is up to you. If you do decide to be there, remember that your ultimate goal is to understand the seller well enough to meet his needs while meeting your own goals.

One thing you need to be careful about is raising your offer dramatically. It makes it appear that you want the home badly and are willing to compromise a lot to get it. If you do raise your offer, it should ideally be tied to getting something in return, perhaps a concession on timing, or payment for roof repairs.

Reaching Your Goals

Whether you choose to be at the meeting where your offer is presented or not, you need to know that this meeting is likely to be the first of many. If you are especially lucky, the seller will accept your offer immediately. He also has the option of refusing your offer unilaterally.

Other options the seller may exercise could be to present you with a counteroffer, or let you know that he has already received another offer that is more attractive than yours (but he is willing to let you revise your original offer). In a really hot market, the seller may announce that he will not respond until a certain time—and he will listen to all incoming offers until that time.

The Counteroffer Dance

Frequently, after he has seen your initial offer, the seller will make a counteroffer. He may accept some, or even most, of the terms in your original offer. But his counteroffer may propose some changes he wants (like more money or removal of a contingency you have placed on the deal).

If you are a single coming out of a marriage and need to sell the house you shared as a married person before you are able to complete the purchase of your new home, you need to be aware that an offer contingent on the sale of your previous home may be unattractive to a seller. In a hot market, he may counter with a clause that gives you a certain amount of time to remove the contingency or the deal is off, or he may reject your offer outright.

In the case of a hot market, you should probably sell your previous home first and then make an offer on a new home. Then you will not only know how much money you have to work with, you will also be in a better position to make a clean, contingency-free offer to a seller when you find an attractive property. This strategy would also be heartily endorsed by anyone in any kind of market who bought a new home without selling the old—and found themselves strapped by two mortgage payments every month until the old home sold.

Get It In Writing

Before you say yes or no, be sure to see the seller's counteroffer in writing. He may use a form supplied by his agent, or it may be less formal. Review each clause of the counteroffer separately. Do any of them affect you in a way your original offer did not? Are those new conditions acceptable to you? If you have any questions, don't be shy about insisting for time for you and your advisors to review the documents.

Be aware that many times the counteroffer can stipulate a deadline by which you have to accept it, make a counter-counteroffer, or the deal is dead. Depending on the stamina and personal aims of the participants, this counteroffer process can go on for days, weeks, or even longer.

Congratulations, It's A Contract!

Once one party accepts all the conditions of the other party's offer, you have a contract. At this point, you will be expected to give the seller's agent a deposit check as discussed earlier in this chapter. When the deal is closed, the money will be applied to the purchase price of your home. The check will be made out to an escrow or title company where the money will be held until the transaction is completed because unfortunately, if the money goes directly to the seller, it can be extremely difficult to reclaim if the deal sours. Even if the deal sours, the escrow holder will probably not refund a deposit to the potential buyer without the consent of the seller—or a court order.

Warming Cold Feet

In the industry, Buyer's Remorse is the term they use for that feeling that you just want to abandon the deal. If you find yourself suffering from buyer's remorse, you are entitled to withdraw from the negotiations—in writing—right up to the moment the seller accepts your current offer in writing.

If you are sure you want to or need to withdraw from the deal, do it in writing immediately and use a method that lays down a paper trail in case you ever need to prove your action. You may choose to fax from a machine that gives you a receipt, a hand-delivered letter where you get a date and signature at delivery or using an overnight delivery service that will get a signed receipt when your notice is delivered.

However, it is much more likely that you and the seller will be able to come to an agreement. While it may be tempting to heave a sigh of relief and think you can relax now, you would be wrong to do it. Now that you have an agreement, you are ready for the next step. Escrow.

9

An Escrow Is Not
A Large Bird

Once you and the seller have come to agreement and you have given your deposit, you are ready to enter escrow. Escrow (called "settlement" in some parts of the country) can seem like some mysterious process, but it is actually more like a breather of sorts. It gives both parties time to do all the things that are necessary to complete the sale while the deposit money and documents related to that sale are prepared and held in trust by an impartial third party and the necessary financing is arranged. Depending on where you live, the third party may be a title company, escrow company, lawyer, real estate broker, or lender who has an escrow department.

How Long Will It Take?

Escrow can last anywhere from a few weeks to much longer, depending on what needs to happen during the escrow period. If it is a very "clean" deal where you have the financing arranged ahead of time, there are no time-consuming contingencies, and the seller is ready to close, it should go fairly quickly.

On the other hand, if you have a clause in your contract stating that you have to sell your old home before you will be ready to close on your new one, escrow could conceivably go on for an indeterminate time. Some of your contingencies may have time limitations that you and the seller have agreed on. For instance, you may have 10 days to arrange to have the roof inspected and decide if you find the report acceptable. As each contingency you have put on the deal is satisfied, you will need to notify the seller in writing. The seller should notify you in writing when each contingency he has put on the sale is removed too.

During the escrow period, you may fulfill the obligations you have under the contract. The obligations can include getting financing, ordering inspections you have requested, or dealing with other conditions in the contract.

At the same time, the seller is handling his obligations. They can include getting a pest or termite inspection and handling his conditions of sale, like finding a new home.

Also during escrow, the parties will order a title search and a new title policy (described in detail below).

When all the conditions of the contract have been satisfied, you will be ready to "close." This is the final transfer of ownership from the seller to you, and it does not occur until after your mortgage has been funded and the deed has been recorded. The term "close" is used as a verb to describe the time when all the details will be completed and the new title recorded, like, "Sally's house will close at noon next Friday."

Before You Close

One thing you will have to take care of before you close is acquiring hazard (or fire) insurance on your new home. The lender will require you have enough of it to cover his financial risk.

In fact, if you do not get this insurance on your own, your lender will get it through his own sources, and it may cost you much more than you would have spent if you had priced the same policy on the open market. Also, the lender will require that you pay for the policy he finds if you have not supplied one of your own. If you do not pay, you will be in default of your mortgage.

The policy your lender requires will be a basic policy to protect him, but many homeowners prefer to go a step further and get a homeowner's policy which will protect them (and their possessions) against a wide range of risks. Each policy has its unique characteristics, but most have certain things in common.

Protecting The Things You Love

In terms of the contents of your home, a homeowner's policy will insure you against the damage, destruction, or theft of your possessions. If you have any especially valuable collections or items, you may need to have a rider put on the policy to cover these items at their full value.

Also, the policy can be written to cover depreciated or replacement costs. If the insurance company is allowed to depreciate the value of your possessions before they pay a claim, you may receive much less than you believe your things were worth (for instance, your seven-year-old stereo may work great—but have virtually no insurance value if it is stolen). A policy that is written to cover replacement value will cost more, but you will be able to replace your things with items of similar value if you have to make a claim.

The best way to guarantee you will receive the maximum benefit available to you under your policy in the event of a claim, is to have proof of your possessions. It takes a bit of time and patience, but you should video tape your home room by room. Open drawers and closet doors, and put out valuables on a table to tape them close up. Be sure to record any serial numbers or other pertinent facts. If video taping is out of the question, ask your insurance agent if he can supply you with an inventory book to record your possessions. When you are done, the tape and/or book should be stored in your safe deposit box or some other safe place away from your property (after all, it's no help if it burns up with other things you own).

While you are thinking about replacement value on your possessions, you might also think about replacement value on your home itself. Whenever there is a major fire or other disaster, there are usually sad stories in the newspaper in the following weeks about homeowners who will not be able to rebuild because they did not have enough insurance.

If the only fire insurance you have is what the lender requires, it will probably not be enough to allow you to rebuild the same size and quality of home you are now buying. Consider getting a policy that will grow with the construction costs in your area—or at least be sure to review your policy every year or two with your agent to be sure you have adequate coverage.

If your new home is in an area identified as a flood plain or subject to earthquakes, you need to talk to your agent to be sure you have a policy which covers those possibilities.

Your homeowner's policy can also include provisions for living costs if your home became uninhabitable for any covered reason (like fire). Those benefits could be used to allow you to live in relative comfort in a hotel or similar situation while your home is repaired.

Your homeowner's policy should also contain liability coverage. If a guest slips on a loose rug and breaks an arm, or your pet bites a neighbor's child, your insurance should cover expenses like doctor and hospital fees as well as any legal awards made against you as a result of litigation on covered matters (minus your deductible and only up to the limit of your policy).

Let's Make A Deal

Finding an insurance agent can be a lot like the process you went through finding a real estate agent—with one major difference. Once you have interviewed several real estate agents, you pick one to work with to help you find a home. With insurance agents, it is completely proper for you to have them bid against each other for your business.

Each one will work to provide you the best policy for you at the best price. And the added benefit for you, is that you can tell each agent what company they are bidding against. Then, they are likely to quickly point out what makes their policy superior to the competition, enabling you to do some serious comparison shopping.

While you are thinking about insurance, you may want to consider whether you want to get insurance to cover your payments in the event that you are not working. As a single, this could be especially important if your income is the only one coming in.

You Can Tell A Home By Its Title

During the escrow period, you will be hearing talk about getting title insurance. You may have automatically expected that when you buy your home, it will come with a clear title and there will not be any nasty surprises about its ownership somewhere down the line. That works most of the time.

Unfortunately, real estate titles may be clouded by various rights and interests including mortgages, liens for unpaid taxes and special assessments, judgments against the current or former property owners, use and occupancy restrictions, mineral rights, and air rights. To protect yourself against problems arising from events that occurred before you bought the property, you should have the title checked professionally and insured.

When you made your offer, it should have been contingent on approval of a preliminary title report. You should get this report from the title company shortly after you and the seller sign the sales agreement.

In Massachusetts, real estate agent Cleve Strong* recently dealt with a situation where he was called on to list a property. The person who claimed to be the seller met him at the home with a key and signed the necessary papers. Strong listed the property, and a buyer was found.

---

* Name changed to provide confidentiality on this case.

In fact, it seemed like this deal was only unusual because of the easy way it seemed to come together. The seller was very agreeable to the buyers' requests, and the buyers had even been able to arrange the closing so they would leave their old home and move into their new home immediately.

Then all heck broke loose. When the attorney for the bank did the title search, he discovered that the seller did not own the property. He was a relative trying to sell the property for the owner whose mental competence was in question—but had not been determined by the courts. The person who originally claimed to be the seller had even forged the seller's name on some legal documents to get the deal as far as it was.

The deal was unsalvageable, and the buyer was left having to move out of his old place without anywhere to go. Strong notes that this kind of situation rarely occurs, but it could happen to anyone. His tip for buyers is to be sure you have left yourself an escape allowing you to remain in your previous home for a while if the deal for your new home should fall through for any reason.

In addition to looking at the title to be sure there are no unexpected encumbrances on the property, you will want to be sure that there are no restrictions that would keep you from fulfilling plans you have for your new home like easements that could keep you from building a pool or adding a room.

According to the American Land Title Association, title insurance in America dates back to 1868, when a Pennsylvania real estate buyer sued a conveyancer—a man he had employed to make a title search—to recover a loss resulting from an error in certification of title. Today, virtually every mortgage bought or sold in the secondary mortgage market is protected by a title insurance policy.

Make It Your Personal Policy

There are two basic kinds of policies, one for lenders and one for buyers. The lender's policy is issued in the amount of a mortgage, and the coverage decreases with the size of the indebtedness as the loan is paid off. The owner's title insurance is issued in an amount equal to the real estate purchase price. Coverage remains in effect as long as you, the insured—or your heirs—retain an interest in that particular property. Inflation riders increase the amount of policy liability as property values go up and are one of the additional coverages available from title insurers.

Unlike homeowner's insurance, there is only a one-time premium at closing for this coverage. If you get both owner's and lender's coverage at the same time based on the same title search, you will probably save money over buying the policies separately.

Why should you get the owner's policy? Sometimes people assume that the lender's title insurance policy will protect their interests. Not so.

For instance, if a utility company decides to exercise a previously undisclosed easement (which the title search missed) and construct a power line through your yard, it can seriously affect your ownership and use of the property without a comparable effect on the lender's security interest. Under the coverage of an owner's title policy, you will be financially protected against loss even if the easement prevails.

An "Ex"-tra Precaution

One problem that comes up from time to time is when a new owner is notified by the seller's divorced spouse that their ex arranged to forge their signature on the deed when the property was sold. Therefore, he or she still has a right to the property. Your title company can investigate these kinds of claims and make any necessary settlements if the claim is valid.

In a case reported by the American Land Title Association, a buyer purchased real estate from heirs named in the will of its deceased owner. Years later, another will of the same owner was discovered which named different heirs. The second will was probated and found to be valid, leaving the buyers with no title to the real estate. The title insurance company protected its insured by paying the full amount of the purchase price as provided in its policy of owner's title insurance.

In another case, a buyer had completed his real estate purchase when a lender with whom he had no previous business relationship unexpectedly filed a lawsuit to foreclose on an unpaid mortgage on the property. The title search of public records had shown that the property had been released from that lien.

After an investigation, it was discovered that the release of the mortgage in the records had been forged, and the mortgage remained binding on the property as the lender claimed. Under the owner's title insurance policy, the title company paid the lender and paid related costs to clear up the problem without any loss to the insured buyer.

It can be tempting to figure that the seller is a good guy, and he would have told you if there were any unrecorded liens on the property, ownership problems stemming from a divorce, or judgments filed against the property, etc. But don't bet your home on it. Considering what you have to lose, title insurance is a great bargain.

In The Abstract

One thing to watch out for are lawyer's "abstracts" letters. This is different from having your lawyer get a title policy for you through a recognized insurer. The abstracts letter means that the lawyer has examined the history of your title and advises you to close the deal based on his opinion. In the event that that lawyer is mistaken, he is the only one you can sue—and he may be dead, bankrupt or in jail if you have to go find him. You could lose everything.

The Cure For Seller's Remorse

On occasion, the seller may change his mind about selling the home or get a more attractive offer after agreeing to your contract. If he tries to back out and return your deposit, he very well may be in breach of contract.

Can you force him to go through with the sale? Probably. If you have opted for arbitration or mediation of disputes in your contract, you will have to pursue that option. Otherwise, you will want to talk with your attorney about filing suit for breach of contract.

If you sue, you can request that the court award you fulfillment of the contract and damages (expenses like storing furniture and costs of living elsewhere) you have incurred in pursuing the suit.

Legal fees can be included if your contract calls for them. Often, just notifying the seller that you will aggressively seek fulfillment of your contract will convince them to complete the sale.

If You Want To Back Out

If you have gotten this far and decide you want or need to back out, the seller can pursue the same remedies against you. As a buyer you have one small advantage. The seller still wants to sell his home and may not easily do that until the situation between the two of you is cleared up.

When you reread your contract, you may discover a clause called "liquidated damages." Technically, liquidated damages means that the seller is entitled to everything you promised under the contract or at least in this clause. In reality, you can often negotiate with the seller for a deal that will enable him to keep some or all of your deposit in exchange for releasing you from your commitment.

Since at the very least, backing out of a deal will cost you significant time and money, you should be careful to only sign contracts on homes you are really willing to buy.

When The Unexpected Happens

Sometimes everything seems to be going along according to plan, when a major monkey wrench suddenly fouls up things. The home could be destroyed by tornado, flood or fire. Maybe the seller drops dead. Maybe she goes crazy. What remedy do you have if things suddenly start spinning out of control?

Some of the problems are relatively simple. If the home you are buying is destroyed, what happens depends entirely on when the destruction takes place. If it is before the close of escrow, it is the seller's problem. Hopefully, her hazard or homeowner's policy was kept in force until the closing and will cover the necessary repairs or rebuilding.

From your standpoint, if this traumatic event has soured you on the deal, you can probably get out of it by not permitting the seller the extension of time she needs to repair the home and deliver it to you in the condition called for in the contract.

115

If the seller dies, things get more complicated. Technically, your contract is enforceable against the estate. In reality, enforcing it may be substantially more trouble than it is worth. You may have to deal with heirs, creditors, and title companies that have become skittish while they determine the status of all the people who may have a claim on the property.

This is a really good time to have a lawyer of your own—preferably one knowledgeable in both real estate and probate. If the situation is simple, perhaps a single heir who will not have to take the property through probate, you may want to continue to pursue the sale.

However, if things are looking too complicated and time consuming, you may want your lawyer to pursue ways of getting you out of the deal (hopefully while having the estate reimburse your deposit and expenses) so you can begin looking for a different home.

Now for the crazy. Unfortunately, the seller who seemed charmingly eccentric can go over the deep end between the time you sign the contract and close the sale. Your best bet here is to have a good real estate agent and access to a great lawyer.

After looking for eight months, Leslie Mohr* in New York State found a three-bedroom classic home. Built in 1925, it had wonderful wood floors and trim, tall ceilings, desirable original fixtures, and a close-in location for her work. What she did not know originally, was that the owner was losing her ability to focus on the deal.

While deciding how much to offer, she consulted with her real estate agent who showed her comparable sales indicating that the asking price might be a bit high. Mohr determined that the property was probably worth between $100,000 and $105,000. The original asking price was $115,000. She bid $100,000 to start with and ended up signing a sales agreement for $105,000.

Now came the frustrating time. When Mohr's engineer was ready to examine the house, suddenly the lockbox (which contained a

---

* Name changed for privacy reasons.

key to the house) on the door disappeared. The owner took it and left a note for the engineer to reschedule.

Mohr consulted her lawyer who advised her not to get too excited or do anything rash. She should reschedule and look to the courts if problems persisted, but her case would be stronger if it did not look like she had been strong-arming the seller.

Mohr tried to reschedule, but the owner was unreachable to all parties (and the lockbox was still gone). Now the problem was that the five-day period the contract allowed the buyer to get inspections done had expired.

Negotiations went back and forth between Mohr, her attorney, and the attorney representing the seller—and the seller kept avoiding everyone. No progress.

Here is where Mohr got lucky. She discovered that the seller had more problems than had been revealed. The home was being put into foreclosure—by two lenders. But even with this incentive and a bona-fide offer, the seller was still behaving strangely.

Before this, Mohr had offered to rent the home before her purchase closed because she was staying with family and was looking forward to regaining her privacy. But her suspicions about how rational the seller was led her to withdraw that offer to protect her own interests.

All this was getting to be too much, and Mohr was considering ways to get free of this deal, but she really did want this home. Mohr's concerns included the possible foreclosure, other potential offers, or unforeseen factors that could ruin the deal. She confesses that she also toyed with the idea of walking from this contract and taking her chances at buying the house on the courthouse steps at the foreclosure sale.

But her sense of fair play kept her from trying to take advantage of the situation. By continually keeping after the people involved, she was able to get the papers signed. Even then, Mohr admits that her problems were not over.

For one thing, there were the utilities. The seller had a troubled history of utility payments that made it difficult for Mohr to convince the utilities that she was a different party and they should connect the utilities for her.

Finally, it looked like Mohr and the seller were going to come face to face at the final inspection before closing. After the interminable stress that had marked the transaction, the seller was waiting at the home when the final inspection was scheduled. Mohr insisted that her agent get the seller out of the house before she did the inspection, and this final step was handled uneventfully.

Almost anti-climactically, the sale closed—and then Mohr took one last precaution since she believed the seller was still not acting totally rationally. She changed the locks and added a new security system the second day she owned the home.

Now Mohr is happily enjoying her home, but she cautions others to be aware that everything may not go quite as smoothly as they hope it will. If things get complicated, you may want to do as Mohr did and work with your real estate agent and lawyer. Perhaps you, too, will eventually get what you want, but you may need a lot of patience and professional help if the seller is mentally unstable.

What's In A Name? (Ways to take title)

Once you have finished negotiating the deal, it can be very tempting to gloss over the questions of how you want to take title and just agree to anything.

However, the way you take title can have a tremendous impact on how you are able to sell the home and what will happen to your equity in the home if you should die. The manner in which your title is vested can also affect real estate taxes, income taxes, inheritance and gift taxes, transferability of title, and your exposure to creditor's claims.

When you talk to your real estate agent or escrow officer, you may have some very specific questions about the pros and cons of various ways of taking title. While these professionals may identify the many methods of owning property, they are not able to recommend a specific form of ownership because that would constitute practicing law. So you may want to consult a real estate attorney who can help you determine the way of title that will best meet your individual needs.

Below are some common ways to taking title as a single adult.

SOLE OWNERSHIP—This manner of taking title can fall into several possible patterns. If you have used more than one name (i.e., if you are no longer using your birth name), you may want to list the name you normally use for business purposes (as on your checks), then you may want to follow it with the term A.K.A. (also known as) and any other name(s) you are known by. As an unmarried adult, you will likely fall into one of two categories:

1. A SINGLE WOMAN/MAN: This is a person who has not been legally married.
2. AN UNMARRIED MAN/WOMAN: A man or woman who was previously married.

CO-OWNERSHIP—If you are considering buying a property with another person, there are several ways you may choose to take title. Each has its own benefits and drawbacks.

1. JOINT TENANCY: This form of vesting title to a property is used by two or more individuals who each receive an equal, undivided, fractional interest in the property. The property is subject to the right of survivorship in that the surviving joint tenant or tenants receive the interest of the dead joint tenant by simply recording proof of death. Title to the property must have been acquired by all joint tenants concurrently, and the document must state the intention to create a Joint Tenancy.

   The benefit to this method of taking title is that it allows the other tenants to take ownership right after a fellow tenant's death, without the hassle and expense of probate. The drawback is that your interest in the property can not be willed to another party.

   Joint Tenancy is often felt to be most attractive to people who are in a committed, long-term (or life-partner) relationship and who want to use this ownership technique to provide for the surviving partner(s) in the event that one partner dies.

2. TENANCY IN COMMON: Using this form of vesting title to a property, you will own an undivided, fractional interest in the property (not a particular part of the property). Your fractional interest is not necessarily equal to the fractional

119

interest of other tenants in common in terms of quantity or duration.

As a tenant in common, you assume a comparable portion of the income from the property. On the other hand, you also bear an equivalent share of the expenses incurred because of the property. As a co-tenant, you may sell or will your share of the property. If you want to provide for your survivor in the event that you die, you may want to put your share into a revocable living trust. If you later decide not to leave your share to your original beneficiary, you can change the name of your beneficiary in the living trust. Of course, if you decide you want the property interest back, you may revoke the trust.

Other Ways Of Vesting Title

For business or personal reasons, you may want to consider vesting title in less traditional ways. Because of the potential for complicated legal ramifications, you must consult an attorney in your state who specializes in real estate law. Below is a selection of ways you may want to consider.

1. A CORPORATION—Created under state law, a corporation is a legal entity that may have one or more shareholders. However, this entity is considered, under law, to have an existence that is separate from the shareholders.

2. A PARTNERSHIP—Under the Uniform Partnership Act, a partnership is considered to be an association of two or more persons who carry on a business for profit as co-owners. The partnership may hold title to real estate in the name of the partnership. Under this type of ownership, the title company may require that you furnish legal documents regarding the nature of the partnership such as corporate articles, bylaws, certificates of partnership and trust agreements.

3. A TRUST—A trust is an arrangement whereby the legal title in your property is transferred to a person called a trustee. The trustee's responsibility is to hold and manage that property for the benefit of the person(s) specified in the trust agreement. This may have special attraction for people who feel responsibility for others (children, aging parents, etc.) who may benefit from this arrangement. Trusts must be crafted for your individual needs and circumstances. There are books you may want to read for background on the subject, and you may want to consult an attorney to ensure your wishes are met by the trust documents you sign.

The information in this chapter is provided to give you some general information about the different ways you may take title to a property. Because of the potential for changes in the law and interpretations of the law from one area to another, you should absolutely consult with an attorney in your area before determining the specific way you should take title to a property, especially if you are considering buying with another person.

10

After The Dance
Is Over

Once you have signed all the papers and received the keys, you have time for a well-deserved rest. For about 30 seconds.

Done? Good! Now it is time to get busy again. You need to be just as careful and concerned about your home now as you were about the negotiations you went through to buy it.

Saving Your Paperwork

In all likelihood, you now have a stack full of papers that rival Mt. Everest. If you do not already have one, now is a good time to get a safe deposit box. Tuck all the papers of a legal nature in there, including your title insurance and hazard insurance policies. You could keep them at home, but if your home burned or were involved in a natural disaster, it could be difficult and time consuming to reconstruct those records for insurance and legal purposes if your original records have been destroyed.

However, you might want to make photocopies of the forms you are putting in your safe deposit box and keep them at home for easy reference if you have any questions later. For instance, if you apply for some kinds of credit, the questionnaire may ask for details about your home purchase. Having copies of the records at home could save you some time in filling those forms out.

Problems In Paradise

No matter how hard you have tried to make everything go smoothly, sometimes problems crop up. Maybe the washer/dryer the seller promised to leave was picked up and shipped by over-zealous moving men. Or the drapes you expected to find in your home have mysteriously disappeared. Perhaps in taking the air conditioner out of the kitchen window, the movers dropped it on the spigot in the sink and broke off the spigot.

If you can imagine a last-minute problem, it has probably occurred to someone. The key is to handle it if it happens to you.

Once you have identified a problem, the first thing to decide is whether it is worth the energy it will take you to run it through channels in hopes of making a recovery. For instance, on the spigot, it may be worth a call to your agent, who can call the mover, who may agree to send a plumber to fix the problem. However, if the seller moved himself, it may be difficult and very time consuming to collect for the costs you incur in fixing the problem. In the long run, it may be easier and cheaper to just replace the spigot yourself. You will be the one who has to decide.

If the problem is something you strongly feel should be remedied by the seller, contact your agent to handle the problem. Most of the time, agents have experience in handling situations similar to yours and can buffer you from the hassle.

In the case of the washer/dryer that was moved against the seller's instructions, the moving company should move it back and re-install it if the instructions were clearly noted by the seller in the mover's contract. Otherwise the seller might find it more economical to simply pay to replace the units.

If your agent fails to get you satisfaction, you have the option of contacting the seller or his agent on your own. You should be very clear on what the problem is and what you expect the seller to do to clear up the problem. You may want to do it in writing to lay down a paper trail in case this problem may result in litigation later.

Now we get down to the serious problems. If you believe the problem involves misrepresentation or other malpractice by the seller's agent, you may want to lodge a complaint with his broker, your state real estate licensing agency, and/or your local Association of Realtors. Because of their Code of Ethics, most Associations of Realtors will be interested in arranging a hearing or mediation to clear up the problem.

When you write to either the state licensing agency or the local Association of Realtors, send a copy of your complaint to the affected agent. He may be more than happy to clear up your concerns in order to protect his license.

If you are doing any of the above, keep good records. You may need them if you eventually decide to file a lawsuit. Keep a phone log (with notes about the conversations you have), copies of letters sent and received, etc.

Finally, if your problem seems too complicated or serious for you to handle alone, hire an attorney.

Don't Sweat The Small Stuff

However, sometimes it helps to step back from your problems a bit and consider how important those problems are to you.

Everyone has heard the phrase, "Don't sweat the small stuff." If the energy you will put into forcing someone else to meet your expectations exceeds the energy you will recoup through the effort, maybe you would be better off to walk away from the problem altogether. You have a new home and new opportunities. You may find you are best served by focusing on those opportunities, rather than the problems. But in the end, only you can decide what constitutes a major problem and what is negotiable.

A Taxing Subject

Certainly, one of the incentives for Americans to buy a home of their own is the ability to tap into substantial tax savings.

How much can you save? A lot.

You can borrow up to a total of $1,000,000 in mortgages on your first and second (vacation) home and deduct the mortgage interest on your federal income tax. A simplistic way to look at it is that if you paid $10,000 in interest on your home in one year and had a tax rate of 28 percent, you would realize a savings of $2,800 in taxes over what you would have paid without this deduction.

In addition, most property taxes can also be deducted—with one caveat. Taxes paid to a state, county, municipality or school district where the funds are used to pay for public works or services are, in all probability, not deductible.

If your tax bill includes special assessments, for things like sidewalks, roads, or landscaping for your own street or neighborhood, you may not be able to deduct those taxes.

However, you should keep those records with your household papers. You may be able to use them to increase the tax basis of your home and reduce your taxable profits when it comes time to sell or trade up.

Another tax benefit is the ability to deduct the points you pay on your new mortgage for the tax the year you take the mortgage out. But only if you are careful. To take advantage of this tax benefit, you have to pay the points out of your own funds—not the proceeds from your mortgage—when you take out the loan.

One more opportunity occurs if you buy your home in conjunction with moving for job-related reasons. Whether you are being transferred or getting a new job, you are eligible to deduct your moving expenses if the distance between your new place of employment and your old home is a minimum of 35 miles farther than the distance between your old job and previous home.

Under these moving deductions, you can write off the cost of trips you make to the area to look for a new home as well as the cost of having your household goods moved and stored. You may also be able to write off expenses for transportation and food/lodging expenses for up to 30 days in your new location if necessary.

CAUTION: Tax regulations change and are subject to interpretation. To get the most up-to-date information and advice on how specific regulations relate to your own situation, you should talk to your personal tax advisor or call the Federal Tax Information and Assistance listed under the Internal Revenue Service in your phone book.

The Basis For Your Basis

As mentioned above, you will need to keep some records to help you reduce any potential future tax liability for capital gains. Simply, your costs for acquiring the home, subtracted from the after-expenses amount you receive when you sell your home equals your gain.

The object is to reduce your gain so that, if you decide to cash out at some future time, you pay the least amount of taxes you legally can.

While you own this home, the thing you need to keep in mind is how you can improve your basis. Your basis is the way of measuring your investment in property for tax purposes. You can use the basis of property to figure the deductions for depreciation, amortization, depletion, and casualty losses. You can also use it to figure gain or loss on sale or other disposition of the property.

You *must* keep accurate records of all items that affect the basis of property so you can make (and if necessary, defend) these computations.

The basis of property you buy is usually its cost to you. Your original basis in property (whether cost or other) must be increased or decreased (adjusted) for certain events. If you make improvements to the property, like adding a pool or a new room, this will increase your basis. If you take deductions for casualty losses, this will reduce your basis.

When you buy real property, certain fees and other expenses you pay are part of your basis in the property. They include:

Assumption of a mortgage: If you buy a home and become liable for an existing mortgage on the property, your basis is the amount you pay for the property in cash plus the unpaid mortgage you assume.

Settlement fees and other costs: Legal and recording fees are some of the settlement fees or closing costs that are included in the basis of property. Some others are:

1. Abstract fees
2. Charges for installing utility services
3. Surveys
4. Transfer taxes
5. Title insurance
6. Any amounts the seller owes that you agree to pay, such as back taxes or interest, recording or mortgage fees, charges for improvements or repairs, and sales commissions

Settlement fees do not include amounts placed in escrow for the future payment of taxes and insurance. The taxes are deducted for the tax year they were paid in. Insurance costs may not be deductible.

Also, if you buy a home and agree to pay taxes the seller owed on it, the taxes you pay are treated as part of the cost. You can not deduct them as taxes paid. If you reimburse the seller for taxes the seller paid for you, you can usually deduct that amount. Do not include that amount in the cost of the property.

Thoroughly confused? Pay your tax advisor for an hour of her time to work out the details of your personal situation. It could be money very well spent.

Decreasing Your Basis

You must decrease the basis of your property by any items that represent a return of capital. If you have a casualty or theft loss, you must decrease the basis of your property by the amount of any insurance or other reimbursement you receive and by any deductible loss not covered by insurance. However, you can increase your basis for amounts you spend after a casualty to restore the damaged property.

On the other hand, you can increase your basis through the costs of improvements that add value to your property, lengthen its life, or adapt it to a different use. For example, putting a recreation room in your unfinished basement, adding another bathroom or bedroom, putting up a fence, putting in new plumbing or wiring, installing a new roof, or paving your driveway are improvements, and their costs are added to your basis in your home. Again, the added value of your basis will enable you to minimize your taxable gain when you sell or trade up.

Perhaps the most important thing to remember, is to keep your records of any transactions that might affect the basis of your home.

If you are not the kind of person who enjoys keeping detailed charts, at least keep a large envelope and put any receipts or records that might possibly affect your basis in there (but be sure to note on them the date, amount, and reason for the receipt—some of the inks used in cash registers, etc., tend to fade). When it comes time to settle out, you can deal with it then, when you are motivated by actually anticipating the tax benefits.

11

Congratulations, It's A Home!

Now that you have the keys, you are ready to move in.

Almost.

There are a few things you need to take care of before you send out the invitations to your housewarming party. If you have never owned a home before, some of those things (like setting up trash collection services) may come as a surprise because in rentals, the landlord may have taken care of them for you.

Turning On Your New Home

It can take some time to make all the arrangements, so you will want to start before the closing. However, arrange for turn-on of services to be the day after closing in case there are problems. If the property does not close, you will have time to call back and delay the turn-ons until you actually own the home.

It may sound silly, but before you can have the utilities turned on, you have to know who to contact. If you are moving within the same community, you probably will be dealing with the same utilities and other services, although there may be some your landlord took care of for you before.

On the other hand, if you are moving to a new community, you may find that you are dealing with a confusing assortment of providers. To determine the ones you need to contact, ask your real estate agent or the sales agent at your new home development for a listing.

You should know that sometimes utilities will ask for a deposit before they will begin your service. This is because they have been stung in the past by customers who have not paid their bills. However, you can often have the deposit waived if you can have your service transferred from your previous address. This may even work if you are transferring from one provider to another. But it will only work if you have regularly paid your bills on time.

While the utilities will need to be changed on a relatively tight schedule, many other changes can be handled much earlier. Once you are in escrow and have a tentative date to close, you will need to start taking care of some time-consuming details. Before you move in, you may want to ask your real estate agent about putting you in touch with any local Welcome Wagon or Newcomer's Club type organizations that can help introduce you to people, organizations, and businesses in your new area.

Planning Chart

Here is a chart to help you handle all the utilities you will need to transfer or turn on for your move. All of them may not apply, depending on the circumstances where you live. There are lines at the end to add any services which are not included on the list.

Service	Date Discontinued At Old Home	Date Begun At New Home
Electricity Company Name:		
_____	_____	_____
_____	_____	_____
Gas Company Name:		
_____	_____	_____
_____	_____	_____
Phone/Local Company Name:		
_____	_____	_____
_____	_____	_____
Phone/Long Distance Company Name:		
_____	_____	_____
_____	_____	_____
Water Company Name:		
_____	_____	_____
_____	_____	_____
Trash/Garbage Company Name:		
_____	_____	_____
_____	_____	_____
Cable TV Company Name:		
_____	_____	_____
_____	_____	_____
Newspaper Publication Name:		
_____	_____	_____
_____	_____	_____
Other		
_____	_____	_____
_____	_____	_____
_____	_____	_____

Keeping In Touch—Current Contacts

In addition to arranging for utility services to be discontinued at your old address and begun at your new home, you will need to change your mailing address with people and organizations you normally do business with. You can fill out your change of address forms at the post office up to a few weeks before your actual move since they have an effective date on them. Once your address has been changed, first class mail will be forwarded for one year, and magazines will be forwarded for 90 days.

Here is a listing of people and businesses you may want to notify of your new address:

CONTACT   DATE NOTIFIED
Post Office   _____
Subscriptions

_____   _____
_____   _____
_____   _____
_____   _____

Physicians/Dentists (For you and/or your children)

_____   _____
_____   _____
_____   _____

Loans (i.e., car or student)

_____   _____

Charge Accounts

_____   _____
_____   _____
_____   _____
_____   _____
_____   _____
_____   _____

Professional Organizations

_____   _____
_____   _____

Social/Service Organizations

_____   _____

Accountant

_____   _____

Bank(s)

_____   _____

_____   _____

Attorney

_____   _____

Stockbroker or Corporations
that mail dividend checks

_____   _____

Government Programs

_____   _____

Insurance Companies

_____   _____

_____   _____

Other (book clubs, frequent flier programs, etc.)

_____   _____

_____   _____

_____   _____

Finally, there are some things you will need to take care of at your new home, especially if you are moving from one area to another.

SUBJECT	DATE HANDLED
Voter Registration	_____
Move Safe Deposit Box	_____
Change Auto Registration (Or at least address)	_____
Get New Driver's License (If necessary)	_____
Register Pets (If necessary)	_____
Register Weapons (If necessary)	_____

Before Your Move

One of the great pleasures of owning your own home is that only you decide how it should look. If you have dealt with landlords for many years, you may be tired of endless white walls and of being forbidden to put a nail in the walls.

When the renovation or redecoration bug bites—it is a good idea to handle as much as possible before actually moving in. Then, if you want to hang wallpaper, build bookshelves, or change the carpets, you can do it without disrupting your life (as in, "I'm running late, what tarp did I put my briefcase under?") or having to move heavy furniture.

One More Thought

One topic that somehow never makes the list of things to do when you are getting ready to move to a new home is the list of people to be invited to your housewarming party.

Depending on your personal style and how you relate to your friends, it could be a formal dinner party, a come-as-you-are-because-we're-going-to-paint-the-walls party, or something somewhere in between.

By the time you have gotten here, you deserve a party. You have earned it. Whether you are celebrating with a barbecue by the pool or throwing yourself a "landscaping plant" shower, take some time to celebrate your achievement.

While singles are about one-third of first-time buyers in today's market, you are a unique person and deserve some recognition for what you have accomplished (and possibly some help getting your place whipped into shape!). Enjoy.

Helping Your Best Friend

Also, be aware that if you have pets, they may need some special handling during the move. You will be distracted with the details that need to be handled, and it can be easy to forget that all this activity is unexpected and confusing to your pet.

Even if you are just moving across town, you may want to board your pet for a few days while the move is going on. Then when you bring your pet home, take some time to play with it and familiarize it with its new territory.

If you have a cat, plan to keep it in for a few days until it accepts its new home. Even if it is normally an outside cat, you may want to litter train it a few weeks before the move and keep it in for a while. Even if your cat is not accustomed to using a leash, you may want to use one the first few times out until your pet is familiar with his territory. Check with local animal control agencies about any regulations which might affect your pet and to see if there are any known illnesses or predators you need to be aware of.

Everyone has heard stories of dogs who limp back to their old home after traveling arduous miles. To prevent that, keep your dog in your new home or yard until he feels at home.

Remember that many communities have leash laws, and in any case, it is rarely considered neighborly to let your dog run loose. If your dog is territorial, you may want to walk the perimeter of your new property with your dog several times to teach him the limits of his territory.

If you have questions about the special needs of your pet, consult your veterinarian with your specific questions. If your pet(s) are tropical fish or other species that you may not have dealt with veterinarians for, contact the expert at your pet shop and ask for information or referrals.

Sometimes, Take Your Time

If you are moving from one community to another, you may also need to transfer memberships in religious, civic, service, and athletic organizations. However, do not be in too much of a hurry. While it is important to let your old organization know you will be moving (and give them a change of address for mailings), you may want to wait before transferring your membership.

There may be more than one religious congregation or chapter of your civic organization within a reasonable distance of your new home. It is a good idea to visit the different choices and get a feel for which ones you are most comfortable with before transferring your membership. The best choice may not necessarily be the one that is geographically closest to your home.

If you have children and they will be changing schools, you need to make both schools aware of your intentions as soon as your plans are finalized. Your old school may prepare a set of records to forward to the new school. If you are moving in the middle of the school year, you might ask your child's teacher to write a letter for the new school outlining his program this year and how far along the class is in that program.

If your child has any outstanding strengths or needs, the teacher may be able to use this letter as a way of introducing those special qualities to the new teacher. When you actually go to the new school to enroll your child, you should also bring a certified copy of the child's birth certificate and a record of your child's health immunizations (you can get that record from your child's doctor or clinic).

Improving Your Investment

Do you see your new home as a temporary residence where you can gain appreciation in value and move up or as a permanent address? In either case, you may be considering making some architectural alterations as a way of making your home more functional and attractive.

If you are going to do this, you should consider the effect your changes will have on the value of your home.

What Is The Payback?

The 1991 Cost vs Value Report is one in a series of annual studies done by *Remodeling Magazine*. These studies take eleven common remodeling projects and compare estimated costs and expected paybacks if the home were to be sold within a year of the remodeling.

Your best bet of jobs that will pay for itself at resale is adding a bathroom to a one or one-and-a-half bath house. Nationally, the average payback is 94 percent. However, the actual payback varies dramatically depending on where you live.

If you are building that bathroom in Honolulu, the job will cost you about $10,200, but when you sell, it will increase the value of your home by $18,200, an increase of 175 percent. On the other hand, if you built the same room in Cleveland where it would cost you about $10,100, you could only expect to receive half of that ($5,000) back in increased value of your home if you sold.

Here are some of the most popular remodeling projects with costs and return on investment for selected cities. Construction costs for each project come from R.S. Means Company, Inc., Kingston, Massachusetts, publishers since 1942 of the annual unit cost estimating books, *Building Construction Cost Data.* The cost estimates assume that the work is done by professional contractors. This information is reprinted with permission of *Remodeling Magazine,* Copyright 1991, Hanley-Wood, Inc.

Remodeling Project	Average Job Cost	Average Resale Value/Percentage	
Major Kitchen Remodel (National)	$19,800	$17,600	89%
Boston	23,200	21,400	92%
Atlanta	17,700	21,400	121%
Cleveland	21,200	16,700	79%
Albuquerque	18,000	10,500	58%

Project Description: Update outmoded 200-square-foot kitchen with design and installation of functional layout of new mid-priced cabinets, laminate countertops, energy efficient oven, cook top with ventilation system, microwave, dishwasher, disposer, and custom lighting. Add new resilient floor, wall coverings, ceiling treatments, and 30 lineal feet of cabinets and counter space, including a 3-by-5 foot island.

Minor Kitchen Remodel (National)	$ 8,000	$ 7,200	90%
Hartford, CT	7,800	8,800	113%
Washington, D.C.	7,700	6,000	78%
Chicago	8,400	10,100	120%
Phoenix	7,300	5,400	74%

Project Description: Refinish cabinets, install new energy-efficient oven and cook top, new laminate countertops and cabinet hardware, wall covering, and resilient flooring, and repaint.

Bath Remodel (National)	$ 7,300	$ 5,700	79%
Philadelphia	7,600	4,800	64%
Austin	6,300	5,600	89%
Wichita, KS	6,200	6,900	112%
Seattle	7,500	5,800	77%

Project Description: Update a 5-by-9 foot bathroom that is at least 25 years old with new standard-size tub, commode, and solid surface vanity counter with two molded sinks. Also install new lighting, mirrored medicine cabinet, ceramic tile floor and walls in tub/shower area (vinyl wallpaper elsewhere).

Bath Addition (National)	$ 9,500	$ 9,000	94%
Garden City, Long Island	11,800	13,800	117%
Dallas	8,300	7,600	92%
Milwaukee	9,200	9,700	106%
Great Falls, MT	8,700	5,200	60%

Project Description: Add a second full bath to a one or one-and-a-half bath house. The 6-by-8 foot bath is within the existing floor plan in an inconspicuous spot convenient to the bedrooms. Includes cultured marble vanity top, molded sink, standard bathtub with shower, low-profile toilet, lighting, mirrored medicine cabinet, linen storage, vinyl wallpaper, and ceramic tile floor and walls in tub area.

Family Room Addition (National)	$29,000	$24,200	83%
Princeton, NJ	30,600	25,900	85%
Knoxville, TN	24,200	13,300	55%
Indianapolis	28,100	27,600	98%
San Francisco	36,200	46,200	128%

Project Description: In a style and location appropriate to the existing house, add a 16-by-25 foot, light-filled room on a new crawl space foundation with wood joist floor framing, matching wood siding on exterior walls and matching fiberglass roof. Include drywall interior with batt insulation; 120 square feet of glass (doors and windows); hardwood tongue and groove floor. Tie into existing heating and cooling.

Sun Room Addition (National)	$18,900	$13,500	71%
Lake Winipesaukee, NH	16,900	17,000	101%
West Palm Beach, FL	16,800	9,200	55%
Chicago	19,800	26,000	131%
San Diego	20,500	23,000	112%

Project Description: Add a 12-by-16 foot living space off the kitchen, dining room, or living room. Custom build on site. Walls and ceiling are mostly insulated glass, tinted or shaded if necessary for climate. Half the windows are operable for ventilation. Includes tile floor and ceiling fan. Tie into existing heating and cooling.

Deck Addition (National)	$ 6,800	$ 4,800	71%
Lancaster, PA	6,800	5,300	77%
Jacksonville, FL	5,700	3,300	58%
Grand Rapids, MI	5,900	4,500	77%
Spokane	6,800	7,400	108%

Project Description: Add a 16-by-20 foot deck of pressure-treated pine. Include a built-in bench, railings, and planter, also of pressure-treated pine.

Master Suite (National)	$22,000	$17,500	80%
Westchester Co., NY	27,500	27,400	100%
Birmingham	18,400	17,500	95%
St. Louis	22,500	18,100	80%
Fresno, CA	23,700	23,300	98%

Project Description: In a house with four or five bedrooms and at least three bathrooms, combine two existing bedrooms and one bath into a master bedroom-bath suite. Involves no load-bearing wall removal and leaves one or two bathrooms near the other bedrooms. Remodel master bath with new fixtures and fittings, tiled floor and shower stall area, separate whirlpool tub, two sinks, and new lighting. Build separate walk-in closet and dressing area.

Replace Windows (National)	$ 6,300	$ 4,300	69%
Pittsburgh	6,300	6,600	105%
Columbia, SC	5,100	3,500	68%
Lincoln, NE	5,500	2,000	36%
Boise	5,900	4,800	81%

Project Description: Replace 16 existing single-pane windows with energy-efficient vinyl or vinyl-clad aluminum double-pane windows.

Replace Siding (National)	$ 8,100	$ 5,200	64%
Ridgewood, NJ	8,500	9,200	108%
Memphis	7,100	3,500	49%
Cincinnati	7,800	7,300	93%
Seattle	8,400	5,100	61%

Project Description: In a neighborhood where siding is appropriate, install 2,000 square feet of vinyl or aluminum siding using 1/4-inch foam insulating board. Include new soffits, fascia, trim, and gutters.

Attic Bedroom (National)	$18,500	$15,600	84%
Providence	18,500	16,300	88%
Louisville	16,500	17,500	106%
Madison, WI	17,100	9,800	57%
San Francisco	23,200	36,200	156%

Project Description: In a two- or three-bedroom house, convert unfinished space in attic with rafters to 15-by-15 bedroom and 5-by-7 foot shower bath. Add four new windows and 15-foot shed dormer. Insulate and finish ceiling and walls. Carpet unfinished floor. Add separate forced air heating and air conditioning. Retain existing stairs.

Protect Your Investment

If you are considering remodeling your home, it is important that you use the same care in choosing your contractor that you would use in choosing any other professional. A bad contractor can leave you with shoddy (or partially done) workmanship, unpaid sub-contractors placing liens on your property, and your money long gone.

When you are looking for a contractor, look for someone with an established local presence and reputation. Interview several and have them go over the details of the project you are planning. Get (and check!) references from each contractor. Also check them out with your local Better Business Bureau and your state licensing agency (if any). One good indicator of a professional is membership in the National Association of the Remodeling Industry (NARI). If you want to call NARI for referral to local members, you can check your telephone white pages under NARI or call (703) 276-7600.

When you have chosen your contractor, get a well-written contract before any work begins or any money changes hands. Your contract should:
1. Itemize what the contractor will and will not do;
2. Specify all materials;
3. Spell out all financial terms;
4. Set a deadline for completion, after which he owes you penalties;
5. Detail any warranties; and
6. Note applicable codes and restrictions and what building permits will be required. You should also get a copy of the contractor's certificate of insurance. Show it to your

insurance agent to be sure you are covered in case of a problem with liability, workman's compensation, etc.

Once the work has started, you will want to check on it from time to time and ask questions about things you do not understand. However, be warned that if you decide to change any details or materials of the remodeling job after the contract is signed, you are likely to have to pay the contractor more money.

12

Finale!

Relax. Now you have learned the basics you will need to know to buy a home and handle the details that will face you. With all the information and programs available to you, buying a home while you're single has never been easier. Whether you buy alone, or go together with another person, you can have a piece of the American Dream if you want it enough to work for it.

To quote a classic statement by Goethe, "What you can do, or dream you can, begin it. Boldness has a genius, power, and magic in it."

Start today to make your dreams of home ownership come true—and Welcome Home!

Glossary

ADJUSTABLE-RATE MORTGAGE (ARM)

A mortgage with an interest rate that is adjusted periodically according to the terms of the mortgage agreement. The amount the interest rate changes is determined by the "index" in the contract and can vary by lender.

AGENCY

The relationship which occurs when a buyer or seller delegates to another (the agent) the right to act on their behalf in a real estate transaction.

ALL-INCLUSIVE TRUST DEED

Sometimes called a wrap-around mortgage. This is a financing tool which creates a new trust deed which includes both the balance due on the existing loan and any new amounts loaned.

AMORTIZATION

The process of gradually reducing the outstanding mortgage loan through regular payments on the principal and interest over a period of time.

ANNUAL PERCENTAGE RATE (APR)

The relationship of the total finance charges to the total amount being financed expressed as a percentage. The finance charges can include interest, service charges, points, loan fees, and mortgage insurance.

APPRAISAL
> The determination of the value of a property by analyzing the facts affecting its market value.

APPRECIATION
> The increase in value of a property.

ASKING PRICE
> The price at which a seller offers a property for sale. Depending on market conditions and negotiations with the eventual buyer, the actual sale price may be higher or lower.

ASSESSED VALUATION
> The value that is attributed to a property by a taxing authority. This value is used to determine the amount of taxes due on the property.

ASSESSMENT
> (1) The amount of taxes attributed to a property, may also include separate taxes for improvements like streets, lighting, sewers, parks, etc. (2) The fee charged by a homeowners association for the owner's share of the association's budget.

ASSUMABLE LOAN
> An existing mortgage that can be taken over by a new buyer. The lender will usually have the right to approve the new debtor before releasing the existing mortgage holder from liability.

ASSUMPTION FEE
> The fee charged by a lender for handling the details involved in processing the paperwork for a new buyer assuming an existing loan.

BALLOON PAYMENT
> The balance of the principal which remains outstanding at the end of the loan. Often part of a short-term loan which is interest only or only partially amortized and has a large lump sum payment due at the end of the term.

BASIS

The original cost for a property plus the amount spent on capital improvements and minus certain losses like casualty losses. The basis is used to determine capital gains on the property.

BINDER

(1) The funds paid by a buyer to a seller to take the property off the market when an offer is made. It is sometimes called "Earnest Money" or "Good Faith Money." (2) A written promise by an insurance company that states that they will insure a certain property.

BREACH OF CONTRACT

When one party to a contract fails to fully fulfill their responsibilities under the contract without legal excuse.

BROKER

A person who is licensed by a state to represent a party or parties in a real estate transaction. A broker may receive a commission or fee for this service. A broker may also supervise real estate agents in his or her office.

BUYDOWN

A payment to a lender to lower the effective interest rate that will be paid by the buyer for a set period of time (often between one and five years).

BUYER'S BROKER

A broker (or the agent working for the broker) hired by the buyer to exclusively represent the buyer's interests in a real estate transaction. The buyer's agent may be paid a commission by the seller or buyer. This agency relationship must be agreed on between the parties, as traditionally the buyer's agent has been a sub-agent of the listing agent. See Chapter 6 for a more detailed description.

BUYER'S MARKET

When market conditions are such that there are more homes available for sale than there are interested buyers, giving the potential buyers a negotiating advantage.

CAP

The maximum amount the monthly payment or interest rate can rise during the life of the loan or any specified adjustment period.

CC&R's

Covenants, Conditions and Restrictions are the limitations placed on owners of real property. These CC&R's are usually enforced by the homeowners association. If a property is subject to CC&R's, that fact must be disclosed to a buyer before the title is transferred. These CC&R's are often found in condominiums and planned unit developments.

CERTIFICATE OF OCCUPANCY

A document issued by a local governmental body allowing people to live in a home.

CHAIN OF TITLE

The chronological recording tracing the title of the land from the original owner to the present owner.

CLEAR TITLE

When the title to a property is free from liens, defects or other encumbrances.

CLOSING

The final procedure when the documents are executed and/or recorded and the mortgage (if any) is recorded. This event is called a "settlement" in some areas.

CLOSING COSTS

Expenses (beyond the selling price) which are paid when the sale documents are executed and/or recorded. These closing costs can include loan fees, title fees, etc.

CLOUDED TITLE

A title that has an outstanding encumbrance of lien which prevents the seller from delivering a clear title and the buyer from purchasing title insurance.

COMMISSION

The money paid to the real estate broker(s) for handling the sale of the property. The commission is usually a percentage of the value of the sale.

COMPARABLE

Comparisons of the prices that similar properties have sold for. Comparables are used both as a tool to help the seller determine the appropriate listing price and as a factor for the buyer to consider in making an offer.

CONDOMINIUM

An individually owned unit in a multi-unit development. The balance of the property (both land and buildings) is owned in common.

CONTINGENCY

A condition on the sale. For instance, a buyer may make their purchase of a house contingent on one or more of a variety of factors including selling a previous home, getting financing, and/or getting an acceptable inspection report on the subject property.

CO-OP

A cooperatively owned property where each owner owns a share of the entire property rather than a specific unit (as in a condominium). While the owner has the exclusive right to use a particular unit, they do not actually own it in the sense of being able to sell the unit. To sell the unit, the owner must sell the share of the company.

CO-SIGNER

A person who signs a promissory note guaranteeing payment by the primary signer.

CO-TENANCY

A general term which covers both joint tenancy and tenancy in common.

COUNTEROFFER

An offer made by a potential buyer in response to an offer to sell. The counteroffer responds by offering the seller a price and/or set of conditions under which the buyer will be willing to buy the property.

DEED

A document which transfers the ownership of a property.

DEED OF TRUST

An instrument sometimes used to replace a mortgage. The property is transferred to a third-party trustee as security for the obligation owed by the borrower.

DEFAULT

The situation where one of the parties to a contract fails to perform their obligations under the contract.

DEFERRED MAINTENANCE

Repairs which are necessary to return a property to good condition. Some homeowners associations may have incurred deferred maintenance because of failure to properly maintain their property.

DEPARTMENT OF REAL ESTATE

The department of state government which is responsible for the licensing and regulations of individuals in the real estate business. Questions and complaints about professionals in the industry can be brought here.

DEPOSIT—See BINDER

DEPRECIATION

Loss in value.

DOWN PAYMENT

The cash amount paid by a buyer toward the purchase price of a property.

DUE-ON-SALE CLAUSE

This is a clause in a mortgage loan agreement which gives the lender the right to demand payment in full when the property changes ownership.

EARNEST MONEY—See BINDER

EASEMENT

A legal right to use another owner's land. Easements are often recorded to allow utilities the right to run electric, phone or cable TV wires, sewers, or pipes through certain parts of a property.

ENCUMBRANCE

This is interest held in a property by someone other than the owner. This encumbrance can be a claim, lien, charge or liability.

EQUITY

The value of a property after existing liens have been satisfied.

EQUITY LOAN

A loan (often a second mortgage) secured by the owner's equity in a property.

EQUITY SHARING

A technique that pairs a cash poor but otherwise well-qualified buyer with an investor who contributes the down payment. At a predetermined future date, the increase in equity is shared using a formula agreed on at the time of purchase.

ESCROW

The process by which a disinterested third party holds all instruments necessary to the sale (including funds and documents) until the deal is closed.

FAIR MARKET VALUE

The price that would probably be negotiated between a willing seller and a willing buyer (neither of whom was under any compulsion to buy or sell).

"FANNIE MAE" (Federal National Mortgage Association-FNMA)

A private corporation which deals in the purchase of first mortgages.

FEDERAL HOUSING ADMINISTRATION LOAN (FHA LOAN)

A loan insured by the Federal Housing Administration.

FHA—See FEDERAL HOUSING ADMINISTRATION

FINANCE CHARGE

A total of all direct and indirect charges as defined by the federal Truth-in-Lending laws.

FIRST MORTGAGE

A mortgage on a property that is superior to any other mortgage on that property. It is also first in line if the property goes into foreclosure.

FIXED-RATE MORTGAGE

A mortgage loan that has a rate of interest that remains the same for the life of the loan.

FORECLOSURE

The forced sale of real estate ordered by a court to pay off a loan that the owner has defaulted on.

"FREDDIE MAC" (Federal Home Loan Mortgage Corporation-FHLMC)

An agency affiliated with the government that buys mortgages on the secondary market from Department of Housing and Urban Development approved mortgage bankers.

FREE AND CLEAR

A real property that has no liens or mortgages against it.

FULL DISCLOSURE

Revelation of all known facts which could affect the decision of a buyer.

"GINNIE MAE" (Government National Mortgage Association-GNMA)

A federal agency, often called "Ginnie Mae," that buys mortgages from institutional lenders.

GOOD FAITH MONEY—See BINDER

GRADUATED PAYMENT MORTGAGE

This mortgage requires increasingly higher payments over the term of the loan. The theory is that the low initial payments will help buyers qualify and the payments will increase (more or less) as the buyer's income increases.

GROSS INCOME

The total income of the buyer(s) before expenses are subtracted.

HOMEOWNERS ASSOCIATION

(1) An association formed by a builder of condominiums or planned developments as required in some states. (2) An association of homeowners in a specific area who have organized for the purpose of maintaining or improving the quality and amenities of the area.

IMPOUND ACCOUNT

An account that is held by a lender. Funds are paid into it on a regular basis to cover the payment of taxes, insurance and other anticipated periodic debts against the property.

INDEX

The published measure of interest rates on certain types of borrowing or investment. Common indexes include the 1-Year Treasury Bill Rate, the 11th District Cost of Funds and the Commercial Bank Prime Rate.

INDEXING

The alteration of a mortgage term, payment, or rate according to a predetermined mortgage-rate index.

INSTITUTIONAL LENDERS

Banks and other lenders that make loans to the public, not including businesses or individuals that make loans to employees.

INSURED MORTGAGE

A mortgage which carries insurance to protect the lender in the event of default by the buyer. This insurance satisfies the balance owing plus costs of foreclosure. These mortgages may be insured by FHA, VA, or independent insurance companies.

INTEREST

The amount paid by the borrower for the use of borrowed funds, usually calculated as a percentage of the total amount due.

INTEREST-ONLY LOAN

A loan that only requires payment of interest during the life of the loan. The principal is then paid back in a lump sum at the end of the loan.

JOINT TENANCY

The undivided ownership in a property by two or more parties. The interests in the property must be equal. If one of the joint tenants dies, that tenant's interest in the property passes to the surviving joint tenants rather than to the heirs of the deceased tenant.

LENDER

A person or entity who loans monies which are repaid. This general term covers all mortgagees.

LEVERAGE

The act of controlling a piece of real estate with a relatively small amount of money. For instance, the down payment leverages the value of the entire property.

LIABILITY

This is a general term which covers all kinds of debts.

LIEN

This is a claim on a property to ensure the repayment of a debt. This claim is recorded against the property as security for the debt. Common liens include mechanic's liens placed by someone who has made improvements on the house or tax liens for situations where the owner has not paid the taxes due.

LISTING

The agreement between the owner of a property and a real estate agent. Under the listing agreement, the agent agrees to diligently attempt to find a buyer for the property who will make an offer that is acceptable to the seller. In that event, the seller agrees to pay a pre-agreed fee or commission.

LISTING BROKER

The broker who signs a contract with a seller to sell the home. This may not be the same person as the seller's agent who may be working for the broker.

LOAN

The general term for the act of lending a principal amount of money to a party who agrees to repay that money along with an agreed upon rate of interest.

LOAN COMMITMENT

This is a written document from a lender (such as a bank or savings and loan) that states that the lender is willing to loan this particular borrower a specified amount of money during a certain period of time.

LOAN ORIGINATION FEE

A one-time fee charged by a lender for the purpose of setting up the loan.

LOAN-TO-VALUE (LTV)

This is a ratio of the amount of a loan to the value of the selling price. It is expressed as a percentage.

MAINTENANCE FEE

An amount charged by homeowners associations in condominium and planned unit developments to cover the expenses of maintaining the common areas.

MARKETABLE TITLE

An unencumbered title to a property that a reasonable buyer will accept.

MARKET VALUE

The price for a property where there is a meeting of the minds. Where a willing buyer will agree with a willing seller on the value of the property with both parties being fully informed.

MORTGAGE

(1) The legal instrument under which a parcel of real estate is offered as security for the repayment of a loan. (2) The act of pledging a parcel of real estate for the repayment of a debt. The borrower keeps possession and use of the property during the term of the loan.

MORTGAGE BANKER

A company that makes mortgage financing using its own funds rather than selling the mortgages on the secondary market. It services its own loans which may or may not be sold on the secondary market.

MORTGAGE BANKERS ASSOCIATION OF AMERICA (MBA)

An organization that represents more than 2,800 mortgage banker firms and corporations.

MORTGAGE BROKERS

A firm or individual who (for a fee) will bring together a lender and a borrower for the purpose of placing mortgage on a piece of real estate. The resulting loans are normally sold on the secondary market and serviced by someone other than the broker.

MORTGAGEE

The lender in a mortgage contract.

MORTGAGOR

The borrower in a mortgage contract.

MULTIPLE LISTING SERVICE (MLS)

The MLS contains information submitted by agents about homes their companies have listed for sale. This information is available in most areas to participating licensed real estate brokers and the agents they supervise.

NATIONAL ASSOCIATION OF MORTGAGE BROKERS (NAMB)

A professional organization that promotes the mortgage brokerage industry by providing educational opportunities. Members adhere to a strict Code of Business Ethics.

NATIONAL ASSOCIATION OF REALTORS (NAR)

The largest trade organization in the U.S. All Realtors are licensed real estate agents, but not all real estate agents are Realtors. NAR members are pledged to a strict code of ethics, preserving the rights of property owners, and maintaining their professional edge through continuing education. Local member organizations may be called Boards of Realtors or Associations of Realtors.

OPTION

An agreement giving the right to buy a property at a pre-agreed price, under pre-agreed terms, during a specified time period. The option holder pays a fee for this right.

ORIGINATION FEE

A fee paid to a lender to process the loan paperwork.

PITI

A lending term referring to the four major components of a normal monthly mortgage payment, Principal, Interest, Taxes, and Insurance.

POINTS

A separate fee charged by a lender to fund a mortgage. One point is equal to one percent of the amount of the loan.

PREPAYMENT PENALTY

A penalty included in a mortgage or deed of trust that becomes payable if the loan is paid off (a) before it is due or (b) within a preset period of the contract such as the first five years.

PRINCIPAL

(1) The amount of borrowed money on a mortgage, not counting interest due. (2) The client of a real estate agent.

PRIVATE MORTGAGE INSURANCE (PMI)

Insurance written by a private mortgage insurance company. It only protects the lender in the event of default or foreclosure—not the borrower.

PROPERTY TAX

A tax levied on real estate based on the value of the property.

REAL ESTATE AGENT

An individual who has met the licensing requirements of his or her state and is qualified to handle real estate transactions.

REAL ESTATE BROKER—See BROKER

REAL ESTATE SETTLEMENT PROCEDURES ACT (RESPA)

A federal statute which requires disclosure to the buyer of specified costs in the sale of residential real estate which is to be financed by a federally insured lender.

REALTOR

A licensed real estate broker who is a member in good standing of the National Association of Realtors and is bound by the NAR's Code of Ethics. The agents or brokers working for a Realtor may be Realtor-Associates and are also pledged to the Code of Ethics.

SECOND MORTGAGE

A separate mortgage which ranks after the first mortgage in priority and would be second in line to be paid off if the property is sold.

SECONDARY MORTGAGE MARKET

Lenders can sell mortgage loans to investors in order to gain an additional supply of money for new loans. Loans insured by FHA or guaranteed by VA and some conventional loans may be purchased or sold by Federal National Mortgage Association (FNMA—sometimes called Fannie Mae). The Federal Home Loan Mortgage Corporation (FHLMC—sometimes called Freddie Mac) purchases conventional mortgages in the secondary market from Department of Housing and Urban Development approved mortgage bankers.

SETTLEMENT—See CLOSING

SHARED EQUITY MORTGAGE—See EQUITY SHARING

TAX LIEN

A lien placed against real estate for nonpayment of taxes.

TENANCY IN COMMON

An undivided ownership in real estate by two or more people. Their interests are not necessarily equal in quantity or duration, and they do not have the right of survivorship.

TITLE

Proof of ownership of a specific parcel of real estate.

TITLE COMPANY

An institution that issues insurance guaranteeing that a person owns the property they bought.

TITLE SEARCH

A search and review of all recorded documents affecting a specific property to determine any and all claims to ownership. The title search is done before issuing a title policy guaranteeing a new owner actually owns the property they have bought.

TOWNHOUSE
>Each unit has its own ground space below and air space above, but may have common walls with other units. Common areas are held in the same manner as condominiums.

UNENCUMBERED
>Free from liens.

UNIFORM SETTLEMENT STATEMENT
>A standard Department of Housing and Urban Development form which must be given to the borrower, lender, and seller at, or prior to, closing the sale.

VA LOAN
>A mortgage loan that is insured and guaranteed by the Veterans Administration. Available to military veterans and some active military who meet certain criteria.

VESTING
>A term describing the way in which title is held, i.e., joint tenancy or tenancy in common.

WARRANTY
>A guarantee (often backed by an insurance policy) that the material and/or workmanship of the home or its systems are free of defects and able to fulfill their function.

Appendix I
Where To Find
Special Buyer's Programs

According to the National Council of State Housing Agencies, the agencies below offer Mortgage Revenue Bond and/or Mortgage Credit Certificate Programs that may enable you to buy a home even though you may feel you are not able to make an adequate down payment or pay market-rate monthly payments.

Call the number for your state or territory to get specific information about the programs available to you.

AGENCY	PHONE NUMBER
Alabama Housing Finance Authority	205/244-9200
Alaska Housing Finance Corporation	907/561-1900
*Arizona Department of Commerce Office of Housing Development	602/280-1365
Arkansas Development Finance Authority	501/682-5900
California Housing Finance Agency	916/322-3991
Colorado Housing and Finance Authority	303/297-2432
Connecticut Housing Finance Authority	203/721-9501
Delaware State Housing Authority	302/739-4263
District of Columbia Housing Finance Authority	202/408-0415
Florida Housing Finance Agency	904/488-4197
Georgia Housing and Finance Authority	404/679-4840

* Arizona and Kansas do not have separate state Housing Finance Agencies.

Hawaii Housing Finance & Development Corporation	808/587-0640
Idaho Housing Agency	208/336-0161
Illinois Housing Development Authority	312/836-5200
Indiana Housing Finance Authority	317/232-7777
Iowa Finance Authority	515/242-4990
*Kansas Department of Commerce and Housing	913/296-2686
Kentucky Housing Corporation	502/564-7630
Louisiana Housing Finance Agency	504/342-1320
Maine State Housing Authority	207/626-4600
Maryland Community Development Administration	410/514-7500
Massachusetts Housing Finance Agency	617/451-3480
Michigan State Housing Development Authority	517/373-8370
Minnesota Housing Finance Agency	612/296-7608
Mississippi Home Corporation	601/354-6062
Missouri Housing Development Commission	816/756-3790
Montana Board of Housing	406/444-3040
Nebraska Investment Finance Authority	402/434-3900
Nevada Housing Division	702/687-4258
New Hampshire Housing Finance Authority	603/472-8623
New Jersey Housing & Mortgage Finance Agency	609/890-8900
New Mexico Mortgage Finance Authority	505/843-6880
New York Housing Development Corporation	212/344-8080
New York State Division of Housing & Community Renewal	212/519-5800
New York State Housing Finance Agency	212/686-9700
State of New York Mortgage Agency	212/340-4200
North Carolina Housing Finance Agency	919/781-6115
North Dakota Housing Finance Agency	701/224-3434
Ohio Housing Finance Agency	614/466-7970
Oklahoma Housing Finance Agency	405/848-1144
Oregon Housing and Community Services Department	503/378-4343
Pennsylvania Housing Finance Agency	717/780-3800
Puerto Rico Housing Finance Corporation	809/765-7577
Rhode Island Housing and Mortgage Finance Corporation	401/751-5566

South Carolina State Housing Finance & Development Authority	803/734-3381
South Dakota Housing Development Authority	605/773-3181
Tennessee Housing Development Agency	615/741-2400
Texas Department of Housing & Community Affairs	512/475-3800
Utah Housing Finance Agency	801/521-6950
Vermont Housing Finance Agency	802/864-5743
Virgin Islands Housing Finance Authority	809/774-4481
Virginia Housing Development Authority	804/782-1986
Washington State Housing Finance Commission	206/464-7139
West Virginia Housing Development Fund	304/345-6475
Wisconsin Housing & Economic Development Authority	608/266-7884
Wyoming Community Development Authority	307/265-0603

Appendix II
Amortization Tables

The following pages contain charts to help you determine what your payments (interest and principal only) would be on loans of varying amounts, lengths, and interest rates.

Your Sunday newspaper real estate section may have charts giving the current interest rates being charged by local lenders, or you can call some lenders and ask what rates currently are. Then use the chart of the interest rate closest to the current rate to estimate what you would pay for different sized loans. Use these charts in conjunction with your financial calculations in Chapter 3.

Buying a Home When You're Single

Monthly Payments for
Interest: 5%   Term (Years)

Principal	5	10	15	20	25	30
1000	18.87	10.61	7.91	6.60	5.85	5.37
5000	94.36	53.03	39.54	33.00	29.23	26.84
10000	188.71	106.07	79.08	66.00	58.46	53.68
15000	283.07	159.10	118.62	98.99	87.69	80.52
20000	377.42	212.13	158.16	131.99	116.92	107.36
25000	471.78	265.16	197.70	164.99	146.15	134.21
30000	566.14	318.20	237.24	197.99	175.38	161.05
35000	660.49	371.23	276.78	230.98	204.61	187.89
40000	754.85	424.26	316.32	263.98	233.84	214.73
45000	849.21	477.29	355.86	296.98	263.07	241.57
50000	943.56	530.33	395.40	329.98	292.30	268.41
55000	1037.92	583.36	434.94	362.98	321.52	295.25
60000	1132.27	636.39	474.48	395.97	350.75	322.09
65000	1226.63	689.43	514.02	428.97	379.98	348.93
70000	1320.99	742.46	553.56	461.97	409.21	375.78
75000	1415.34	795.49	593.10	494.97	438.44	402.62
80000	1509.70	848.52	632.63	527.96	467.67	429.46
85000	1604.05	901.56	672.17	560.96	496.90	456.30
90000	1698.41	954.59	711.71	593.96	526.13	483.14
95000	1792.77	1007.62	751.25	626.96	555.36	509.98
100000	1887.12	1060.66	790.79	659.96	584.59	536.82
105000	1981.48	1113.69	830.33	692.95	613.82	563.66
110000	2075.84	1166.72	869.87	725.95	643.05	590.50
115000	2170.19	1219.75	909.41	758.95	672.28	617.34
120000	2264.55	1272.79	948.95	791.95	701.51	644.19
125000	2358.90	1325.82	988.49	824.94	730.74	671.03
130000	2453.26	1378.85	1028.03	857.94	759.97	697.87
135000	2547.62	1431.88	1067.57	890.94	789.20	724.71
140000	2641.97	1484.92	1107.11	923.94	818.43	751.55
145000	2736.33	1537.95	1146.65	956.94	847.66	778.39
150000	2830.69	1590.98	1186.19	989.93	876.89	805.23
155000	2925.04	1644.02	1225.73	1022.93	906.11	832.07
160000	3019.40	1697.05	1265.27	1055.93	935.34	858.91
165000	3113.75	1750.08	1304.81	1088.93	964.57	885.76
170000	3208.11	1803.11	1344.35	1121.92	993.80	912.60
175000	3302.47	1856.15	1383.89	1154.92	1023.23	939.44
180000	3396.82	1909.18	1423.43	1187.92	1052.26	966.28
185000	3491.18	1962.21	1462.97	1220.92	1081.49	993.12
190000	3585.53	2015.24	1502.51	1253.92	1110.72	1019.96
195000	3679.89	2068.28	1542.05	1286.91	1139.95	1046.80
200000	3774.25	2121.31	1581.59	1319.91	1169.18	1073.64
205000	3868.60	2174.34	1621.13	1352.91	1198.41	1100.48
210000	3962.96	2227.38	1660.67	1385.91	1227.64	1127.33
215000	4057.32	2280.41	1700.21	1418.90	1256.87	1154.17
220000	4151.67	2333.44	1739.75	1451.90	1286.10	1181.01
225000	4246.03	2386.47	1779.29	1484.90	1315.33	1207.85
230000	4340.38	2439.51	1818.83	1517.90	1344.56	1234.69
235000	4434.74	2492.54	1858.37	1550.90	1373.79	1261.53
240000	4529.10	2545.57	1897.90	1583.89	1403.02	1288.37
245000	4623.45	2598.61	1937.44	1616.89	1432.25	1315.21
250000	4717.81	2651.64	1976.98	1649.89	1461.48	1342.05

Monthly Payments for
Interest: 5.5%

Principal	5	10	Term (Years) 15	20	25	30
1000	19.10	10.85	8.17	6.88	6.14	5.68
5000	95.51	54.26	40.85	34.39	30.70	28.39
10000	191.01	108.53	81.71	68.79	61.41	56.78
15000	286.52	162.79	122.56	103.18	92.11	85.17
20000	382.02	217.05	163.42	137.58	122.82	113.56
25000	477.53	271.32	204.27	171.97	153.52	141.95
30000	573.03	325.58	245.13	206.37	184.23	170.34
35000	668.54	379.84	285.98	240.76	214.93	198.73
40000	764.05	434.11	326.83	275.15	245.63	227.12
45000	859.55	488.37	367.69	309.55	276.34	255.51
50000	955.06	542.63	408.84	343.94	307.04	283.89
55000	1050.56	596.89	449.40	378.34	337.75	312.28
60000	1146.07	651.16	490.25	412.73	368.45	340.67
65000	1241.58	705.42	531.10	447.13	399.16	369.06
70000	1337.08	759.68	571.96	481.52	429.86	397.45
75000	1432.59	813.95	612.81	515.92	460.57	425.84
80000	1528.09	868.21	653.67	550.31	491.27	454.23
85000	1623.60	922.47	694.52	584.70	521.97	482.62
90000	1719.10	976.74	735.38	619.10	552.68	511.01
95000	1814.61	1031.00	776.23	653.49	583.38	539.40
100000	1910.12	1085.26	817.08	687.89	614.09	567.79
105000	2005.62	1139.53	857.94	722.28	644.79	596.18
110000	2101.13	1193.79	898.79	756.68	675.50	624.57
115000	2196.63	1248.05	939.65	791.07	706.20	652.96
120000	2292.14	1302.32	980.50	825.46	736.90	681.35
125000	2387.65	1356.58	1021.35	859.86	767.61	709.74
130000	2483.15	1410.84	1062.21	894.25	798.31	738.13
135000	2578.66	1465.10	1103.06	928.65	829.02	766.52
140000	2674.16	1519.37	1143.93	963.04	859.72	794.90
145000	2769.67	1573.63	1184.77	997.44	890.43	823.29
150000	2865.17	1627.89	1225.63	1031.83	921.13	851.68
155000	2960.68	1682.16	1266.48	1066.23	951.84	880.07
160000	3056.19	1736.42	1307.33	1100.62	982.54	908.46
165000	3151.69	1790.68	1348.19	1135.01	1013.24	936.85
170000	3247.20	1844.95	1389.04	1169.41	1043.95	965.24
175000	3342.70	1899.21	1429.90	1203.80	1074.65	993.63
180000	3438.21	1953.47	1470.75	1238.20	1105.36	1022.02
185000	3533.72	2007.74	1511.60	1272.59	1136.06	1050.41
190000	3629.22	2062.00	1552.46	1306.99	1166.77	1078.80
195000	3724.73	2116.26	1593.31	1341.38	1197.47	1107.19
200000	3820.23	2170.53	1634.17	1375.77	1228.17	1135.58
205000	3915.74	2224.79	1675.02	1410.17	1258.88	1163.97
210000	4011.24	2279.05	1715.88	1444.56	1289.58	1192.36
215000	4106.75	2333.31	1756.73	1478.96	1320.29	1220.75
220000	4202.26	2387.58	1797.58	1513.35	1350.99	1249.14
225000	4297.76	2441.84	1838.44	1547.75	1381.70	1277.53
230000	4393.27	2496.10	1879.29	1582.14	1412.40	1305.91
235000	4488.77	2550.37	1920.15	1616.54	1443.11	1334.30
240000	4584.28	2604.63	1961.00	1650.93	1473.81	1362.69
245000	4679.78	2658.89	2001.85	1685.32	1504.51	1391.08
250000	4775.29	2713.16	2042.71	1719.72	1535.22	1419.47

Monthly Payments for
Interest: 6%

Principal	5	10	Term (Years) 15	20	25	30
1000	19.33	11.10	8.44	7.16	6.44	6.00
5000	96.66	55.51	42.19	35.82	32.22	29.98
10000	193.33	111.02	84.39	71.64	64.43	59.96
15000	289.99	166.53	126.58	107.46	96.65	89.93
20000	386.66	222.04	168.77	143.29	128.86	119.91
25000	483.32	277.55	210.96	179.11	161.08	149.89
30000	579.98	333.06	253.16	214.93	193.29	179.87
35000	676.65	388.57	295.35	250.75	225.51	209.84
40000	773.31	444.08	337.54	286.57	257.72	239.82
45000	869.98	499.59	379.74	322.39	289.94	269.80
50000	966.64	555.10	421.93	358.22	322.15	299.78
55000	1063.30	610.61	464.12	394.04	354.37	329.75
60000	1159.97	666.12	506.31	429.86	386.58	359.73
65000	1256.63	721.63	548.51	465.68	418.80	389.71
70000	1353.30	777.14	590.70	501.50	451.01	419.69
75000	1449.96	832.65	632.89	537.32	483.23	449.66
80000	1546.62	888.16	675.09	573.14	515.44	479.64
85000	1643.29	943.67	717.28	608.97	547.66	509.62
90000	1739.95	999.18	759.47	644.79	579.87	539.60
95000	1836.62	1054.69	801.66	680.61	612.09	569.57
100000	1933.28	1110.21	843.86	716.43	644.30	599.55
105000	2029.94	1165.72	886.05	752.25	676.52	629.53
110000	2126.61	1221.23	928.24	788.07	708.73	659.51
115000	2223.27	1276.74	970.44	823.90	740.95	689.48
120000	2319.94	1332.25	1012.63	859.72	773.16	719.46
125000	2416.60	1387.76	1054.82	895.54	805.38	749.44
130000	2513.26	1443.27	1097.01	931.36	837.59	779.42
135000	2609.93	1498.78	1139.21	967.18	869.81	809.39
140000	2706.59	1554.29	1181.40	1003.00	902.02	839.37
145000	2803.26	1609.80	1223.59	1038.83	934.24	869.35
150000	2899.92	1665.31	1265.79	1074.65	966.45	899.33
155000	2996.58	1720.82	1307.98	1110.47	998.67	929.30
160000	3093.25	1776.33	1350.17	1146.29	1030.88	959.28
165000	3189.91	1831.84	1392.36	1182.11	1063.10	989.26
170000	3286.58	1887.35	1434.56	1217.93	1095.31	1019.24
175000	3383.24	1942.86	1476.75	1253.75	1127.53	1049.21
180000	3479.90	1998.37	1518.94	1289.58	1159.74	1079.19
185000	3576.57	2053.88	1561.14	1325.40	1191.96	1109.17
190000	3673.23	2109.39	1603.33	1361.22	1224.17	1139.15
195000	3769.90	2164.90	1645.52	1397.04	1256.39	1169.12
200000	3866.56	2220.41	1687.71	1432.86	1288.60	1199.10
205000	3963.22	2275.92	1729.91	1468.68	1320.82	1229.08
210000	4059.89	2331.43	1772.10	1504.51	1353.03	1259.06
215000	4156.55	2386.94	1814.29	1540.33	1385.25	1289.03
220000	4253.22	2442.45	1856.49	1576.15	1417.46	1319.01
225000	4349.88	2497.96	1898.68	1611.97	1449.68	1348.99
230000	4446.54	2553.47	1940.87	1647.79	1481.89	1378.97
235000	4543.21	2608.98	1983.06	1683.61	1514.11	1408.94
240000	4639.87	2664.49	2025.26	1719.43	1546.32	1438.92
245000	4736.54	2720.00	2067.45	1755.26	1578.54	1468.90
250000	4833.20	2775.51	2109.64	1791.08	1610.75	1498.88

Monthly Payments for
Interest: 6.5%   Term (Years)

Principal	5	10	15	20	25	30
1000	19.57	11.35	8.71	7.46	6.75	6.32
5000	97.83	56.77	43.56	37.28	33.76	31.60
10000	195.66	113.55	87.11	74.56	67.52	63.21
15000	293.49	170.32	130.67	111.84	101.28	94.81
20000	391.32	227.10	174.22	149.11	135.04	126.41
25000	489.15	283.87	217.78	186.39	168.80	158.02
30000	586.98	340.64	261.33	223.67	202.56	189.62
35000	684.82	397.42	304.89	260.95	236.32	221.22
40000	782.65	454.19	348.44	298.23	270.08	252.83
45000	880.48	510.97	392.00	335.51	303.84	284.43
50000	978.31	567.74	435.55	372.79	337.60	316.03
55000	1076.14	624.51	479.11	410.07	371.36	347.64
60000	1173.97	681.29	522.66	447.34	405.12	379.24
65000	1271.80	738.06	566.22	484.62	438.88	410.84
70000	1369.63	794.84	609.78	521.90	472.65	442.45
75000	1467.46	851.61	653.33	559.18	506.41	474.05
80000	1565.29	908.38	696.89	596.46	540.17	505.65
85000	1663.12	965.16	740.44	633.74	573.93	537.26
90000	1760.95	1021.93	784.00	671.02	607.69	568.86
95000	1858.78	1078.71	827.55	708.29	641.45	600.46
100000	1956.61	1135.48	871.11	745.57	675.21	632.07
105000	2054.45	1192.25	914.66	782.85	708.97	663.67
110000	2152.28	1249.03	958.22	820.13	742.73	695.27
115000	2250.11	1305.80	1001.77	857.41	776.49	726.88
120000	2347.94	1362.58	1045.33	894.69	810.25	758.48
125000	2445.77	1419.35	1088.88	931.97	844.01	790.09
130000	2543.60	1476.12	1132.44	969.25	877.77	821.69
135000	2641.43	1532.90	1175.99	1006.52	911.53	853.29
140000	2739.26	1589.67	1219.55	1043.80	945.29	884.90
145000	2837.09	1646.45	1263.11	1081.08	979.05	916.50
150000	2934.92	1703.22	1306.66	1118.36	1012.81	948.10
155000	3032.75	1759.99	1350.22	1155.64	1046.57	979.71
160000	3130.58	1816.77	1393.77	1192.92	1080.33	1011.31
165000	3228.41	1873.54	1437.33	1230.20	1114.09	1042.91
170000	3326.25	1930.32	1480.88	1267.47	1147.85	1074.52
175000	3424.08	1987.09	1524.44	1304.75	1181.61	1106.12
180000	3521.91	2043.86	1567.09	1342.03	1215.37	1137.72
185000	3619.74	2100.64	1611.55	1379.31	1249.13	1169.33
190000	3717.57	2157.41	1655.10	1416.59	1282.89	1200.93
195000	3815.40	2214.19	1698.66	1453.87	1316.65	1232.53
200000	3913.23	2270.96	1742.21	1491.15	1350.41	1264.14
205000	4011.06	2327.73	1785.77	1528.42	1384.17	1295.74
210000	4108.89	2384.51	1829.33	1565.70	1417.94	1327.34
215000	4206.72	2441.28	1872.88	1602.98	1451.70	1358.95
220000	4304.55	2498.06	1916.44	1640.26	1485.46	1390.55
225000	4402.38	2554.83	1959.99	1677.54	1519.22	1422.15
230000	4500.21	2611.60	2003.55	1714.82	1552.98	1453.76
235000	4598.04	2668.38	2047.10	1752.10	1586.74	1485.36
240000	4695.88	2725.15	2090.66	1789.38	1620.50	1516.96
245000	4793.71	2781.93	2134.21	1826.65	1654.26	1548.57
250000	4891.54	2838.70	2177.77	1863.93	1688.02	1580.17

Monthly Payments for
Interest: 7%

Principal	5	10	Term (Years) 15	20	25	30
1000	19.80	11.61	8.99	7.75	7.07	6.65
5000	99.01	58.05	44.94	38.76	35.34	33.27
10000	198.01	116.11	89.88	77.53	70.68	66.53
15000	297.02	174.16	134.82	116.29	106.02	99.80
20000	396.02	232.22	179.77	155.06	141.36	133.06
25000	495.03	290.27	224.71	193.82	176.69	166.33
30000	594.04	348.33	269.65	232.59	212.03	199.59
35000	693.04	406.38	314.59	271.35	247.37	232.86
40000	792.05	464.43	359.53	310.12	282.71	266.12
45000	891.05	522.49	404.47	348.88	318.05	299.39
50000	990.06	580.54	449.41	387.65	353.39	332.65
55000	1089.07	638.60	494.36	426.41	388.73	365.92
60000	1188.07	696.65	539.30	465.18	424.07	399.18
65000	1287.08	754.71	584.24	503.94	459.41	432.45
70000	1386.08	812.76	629.18	542.71	494.75	465.71
75000	1485.09	870.81	674.12	581.47	530.08	498.98
80000	1584.10	928.87	719.06	620.24	565.42	532.24
85000	1683.10	986.92	764.00	659.00	600.76	565.51
90000	1782.11	1044.98	808.95	697.77	636.10	598.77
95000	1881.11	1103.03	853.89	736.53	671.44	632.04
100000	1980.12	1161.08	898.83	775.30	706.78	665.30
105000	2079.13	1219.14	943.77	814.06	742.12	698.57
110000	2178.13	1277.19	988.71	852.83	777.46	731.83
115000	2277.14	1335.25	1033.65	891.59	812.80	765.10
120000	2376.14	1393.30	1078.59	930.36	848.14	798.36
125000	2475.15	1451.36	1123.54	969.12	883.47	831.63
130000	2574.16	1509.41	1168.48	1007.89	918.81	864.89
135000	2673.16	1567.46	1213.42	1046.65	954.15	898.16
140000	2772.17	1625.52	1258.36	1085.42	989.49	931.42
145000	2871.17	1683.57	1303.30	1124.18	1024.83	964.69
150000	2970.18	1741.63	1348.24	1162.95	1060.17	997.95
155000	3069.19	1799.68	1393.18	1201.71	1095.51	1031.22
160000	3168.19	1857.74	1438.13	1240.48	1130.85	1064.48
165000	3267.20	1915.79	1483.07	1279.24	1166.19	1097.75
170000	3366.20	1973.84	1528.01	1318.01	1201.52	1131.01
175000	3465.21	2031.90	1572.95	1356.77	1236.86	1164.28
180000	3564.22	2089.95	1617.89	1395.54	1272.20	1197.54
185000	3663.22	2148.01	1662.83	1434.30	1307.54	1230.81
190000	3762.23	2206.06	1707.77	1473.07	1342.88	1264.07
195000	3861.23	2264.12	1752.72	1511.83	1378.22	1297.34
200000	3960.24	2322.17	1797.66	1550.60	1413.56	1330.60
205000	4059.25	2380.22	1842.60	1589.36	1448.90	1363.87
210000	4158.25	2438.28	1887.54	1628.13	1484.24	1397.14
215000	4257.26	2496.33	1932.48	1666.89	1519.58	1430.40
220000	4356.26	2554.39	1977.42	1705.66	1554.91	1463.67
225000	4455.27	2612.44	2022.36	1744.42	1590.25	1496.93
230000	4554.28	2670.50	2067.31	1783.19	1625.59	1530.20
235000	4653.28	2728.55	2112.25	1821.95	1660.93	1563.46
240000	4752.29	2786.60	2157.19	1860.72	1696.27	1596.73
245000	4851.29	2844.66	2202.13	1899.48	1731.61	1629.99
250000	4950.30	2902.71	2247.07	1938.25	1766.95	1663.26

Appendix II — Amortization Tables

Principal	5	10	Term (Years) 15	20	25	30
1000	20.04	11.87	9.27	8.06	7.39	6.99
5000	100.19	59.35	46.35	40.28	36.95	34.96
10000	200.38	118.70	92.70	80.56	73.90	69.92
15000	300.57	178.05	139.05	120.84	110.85	104.88
20000	400.76	237.40	185.40	161.12	147.80	139.84
25000	500.95	296.75	231.75	201.40	184.75	174.80
30000	601.14	356.11	278.10	241.68	221.70	209.76
35000	701.33	415.46	324.45	281.96	258.65	244.73
40000	801.52	474.81	370.80	322.24	295.60	279.69
45000	901.71	534.16	417.16	362.52	332.55	314.65
50000	1001.90	593.51	463.51	402.80	369.50	349.61
55000	1102.09	652.86	509.86	443.08	406.45	384.57
60000	1202.28	712.21	556.21	483.36	443.39	419.53
65000	1302.47	771.56	602.56	523.64	480.34	454.49
70000	1402.66	830.91	648.91	563.92	517.29	489.45
75000	1502.85	890.26	695.26	604.19	554.24	524.41
80000	1603.04	949.61	741.61	644.47	591.19	559.37
85000	1703.23	1008.97	787.96	684.75	628.14	594.33
90000	1803.42	1068.32	834.31	725.03	665.09	629.29
95000	1903.61	1127.67	880.66	765.31	702.04	664.25
100000	2003.79	1187.02	927.01	805.59	738.99	699.21
105000	2103.98	1246.37	973.36	845.87	775.94	734.18
110000	2204.17	1305.72	1019.71	886.15	812.89	769.14
115000	2304.36	1365.07	1066.06	926.43	849.84	804.10
120000	2404.55	1424.42	1112.41	966.71	886.79	839.06
125000	2504.74	1483.77	1158.77	1006.99	923.74	874.02
130000	2604.93	1543.12	1205.12	1047.27	960.69	908.98
135000	2705.12	1602.47	1251.47	1087.55	997.64	943.94
140000	2805.31	1661.82	1297.82	1127.83	1034.59	978.90
145000	2905.50	1721.18	1344.17	1168.11	1071.54	1013.86
150000	3005.69	1780.53	1390.52	1208.39	1108.49	1048.82
155000	3105.88	1839.88	1436.87	1248.67	1145.44	1083.78
160000	3206.07	1899.23	1483.22	1288.95	1182.39	1118.74
165000	3306.26	1958.58	1529.57	1329.23	1219.34	1153.70
170000	3406.45	2017.93	1575.92	1369.51	1256.29	1188.66
175000	3506.64	2077.28	1622.27	1409.79	1293.23	1223.63
180000	3606.83	2136.63	1668.62	1450.07	1330.18	1258.59
185000	3707.02	2195.98	1714.97	1490.35	1367.13	1293.55
190000	3807.21	2255.33	1761.32	1530.63	1404.08	1328.51
195000	3907.40	2314.68	1807.67	1570.91	1441.03	1363.47
200000	4007.59	2374.04	1854.02	1611.19	1477.98	1398.43
205000	4107.78	2433.39	1900.38	1651.47	1514.93	1433.39
210000	4207.97	2492.74	1946.73	1691.75	1551.88	1468.35
215000	4308.16	2552.09	1993.08	1732.03	1588.83	1503.31
220000	4408.35	2611.44	2039.43	1772.31	1625.78	1538.27
225000	4508.54	2670.79	2085.78	1812.58	1662.73	1573.23
230000	4608.73	2730.14	2132.13	1852.86	1699.68	1608.19
235000	4708.92	2789.49	2178.48	1893.14	1736.63	1643.15
240000	4809.11	2848.84	2224.83	1933.42	1773.58	1678.11
245000	4909.30	2908.19	2271.18	1973.70	1810.53	1713.08
250000	5009.49	2967.54	2317.53	2013.98	1847.48	1748.04

Buying a Home When You're Single

Monthly Payments for
Interest: 8 %   Term (Years)

Principal	5	10	15	20	25	30
1000	20.28	12.13	9.56	8.36	7.72	7.34
5000	101.38	60.66	47.78	41.82	38.59	36.69
10000	202.76	121.33	95.57	83.64	77.18	73.38
15000	304.15	181.99	143.35	125.47	115.77	110.06
20000	405.53	242.66	191.13	167.29	154.36	146.75
25000	506.91	303.32	238.91	209.11	192.95	183.44
30000	608.29	363.98	286.70	250.93	231.54	220.13
35000	709.67	424.65	334.48	292.75	270.14	256.82
40000	811.06	485.31	382.26	334.58	308.73	293.51
45000	912.44	545.97	430.04	376.40	347.32	330.19
50000	1013.82	606.64	477.83	418.22	385.91	366.88
55000	1115.20	667.30	525.61	460.04	424.50	403.57
60000	1216.58	727.97	573.39	501.86	463.09	440.26
65000	1317.97	788.63	621.17	543.69	501.68	476.95
70000	1419.35	849.29	668.96	585.51	540.27	513.64
75000	1520.73	909.96	716.74	627.33	578.86	550.32
80000	1622.11	970.62	764.52	669.15	617.45	587.01
85000	1723.49	1031.28	812.30	710.97	656.04	623.70
90000	1824.88	1091.95	860.09	752.80	694.63	660.39
95000	1926.26	1152.61	907.87	794.62	733.23	697.08
100000	2027.64	1213.28	955.65	836.44	771.82	733.76
105000	2129.02	1273.94	1003.43	878.26	810.41	770.45
110000	2230.40	1334.60	1051.22	920.08	849.00	807.14
115000	2331.79	1395.27	1099.00	961.91	887.59	843.83
120000	2433.17	1455.93	1146.78	1003.73	926.18	880.52
125000	2534.55	1516.59	1194.57	1045.55	964.77	917.21
130000	2635.93	1577.26	1242.35	1087.37	1003.36	953.89
135000	2737.31	1637.92	1290.13	1129.19	1041.95	990.58
140000	2838.70	1698.59	1337.91	1171.02	1080.54	1027.27
145000	2940.08	1759.25	1385.70	1212.84	1119.13	1063.96
150000	3041.46	1819.91	1433.48	1254.66	1157.72	1100.65
155000	3142.84	1880.58	1481.26	1296.48	1196.32	1137.34
160000	3244.22	1941.24	1529.04	1338.30	1234.91	1174.02
165000	3345.61	2001.91	1576.83	1380.13	1273.50	1210.71
170000	3446.99	2062.57	1624.61	1421.95	1312.09	1247.40
175000	3548.37	2123.23	1672.39	1463.77	1350.68	1284.09
180000	3649.75	2183.90	1720.17	1505.59	1389.27	1320.78
185000	3751.13	2244.56	1767.96	1547.41	1427.86	1357.46
190000	3852.51	2305.22	1815.74	1589.24	1466.45	1394.15
195000	3953.90	2365.89	1863.52	1631.06	1505.04	1430.84
200000	4055.28	2426.55	1911.30	1672.88	1543.63	1467.53
205000	4156.66	2487.22	1959.09	1714.70	1582.22	1504.22
210000	4258.04	2547.88	2006.87	1756.52	1620.81	1540.91
215000	4359.42	2608.54	2054.65	1798.35	1659.40	1577.59
220000	4460.81	2669.21	2102.43	1840.17	1698.00	1614.28
225000	4562.19	2729.87	2150.22	1881.99	1736.59	1650.97
230000	4663.57	2790.53	2198.00	1923.81	1775.18	1687.66
235000	4764.95	2851.20	2245.78	1965.63	1813.77	1724.35
240000	4866.33	2911.86	2293.57	2007.46	1852.36	1761.03
245000	4967.72	2972.53	2341.35	2049.28	1890.95	1797.72
250000	5069.10	3033.19	2389.13	2091.10	1929.54	1834.41

Appendix II — Amortization Tables

Monthly Payments for
Interest: 8.5 %
Term (Years)

Principal	5	10	15	20	25	30
1000	20.52	12.40	9.85	8.68	8.05	7.69
5000	102.58	61.99	49.24	43.39	40.26	38.45
10000	205.17	123.99	98.47	86.78	80.52	76.89
15000	307.75	185.98	147.71	130.17	120.78	115.34
20000	410.33	247.97	196.95	173.56	161.05	153.78
25000	512.91	309.96	246.18	216.96	201.31	192.23
30000	615.50	371.96	295.42	260.35	241.57	230.67
35000	718.08	433.95	344.66	303.74	281.83	269.12
40000	820.66	495.94	393.90	347.13	322.09	307.57
45000	923.24	557.94	443.13	390.52	362.35	346.01
50000	1025.83	619.93	492.37	433.91	402.61	384.46
55000	1128.41	681.92	541.61	477.30	442.87	422.90
60000	1230.99	743.91	590.84	520.69	483.14	461.35
65000	1333.57	805.91	640.08	564.09	523.40	499.79
70000	1436.16	867.90	689.32	607.48	563.66	538.24
75000	1538.74	929.89	738.55	650.87	603.92	576.69
80000	1641.32	991.89	787.79	694.26	644.18	615.13
85000	1743.91	1053.88	837.03	737.65	684.44	653.58
90000	1846.49	1115.87	886.27	781.04	724.70	692.02
95000	1949.07	1177.86	935.50	824.43	764.97	730.47
100000	2051.65	1239.86	984.74	867.82	805.23	768.91
105000	2154.24	1301.85	1033.98	911.21	845.49	807.36
110000	2256.82	1363.84	1083.21	954.61	885.75	845.80
115000	2359.40	1425.84	1132.45	998.00	926.01	884.25
120000	2461.98	1487.83	1181.69	1041.39	966.27	922.70
125000	2564.57	1549.82	1230.92	1084.78	1006.53	961.14
130000	2667.15	1611.81	1280.16	1128.17	1046.80	999.59
135000	2769.73	1673.81	1329.40	1171.56	1087.06	1038.03
140000	2872.31	1735.80	1378.64	1214.95	1127.32	1076.48
145000	2974.90	1797.79	1427.87	1258.34	1167.58	1114.92
150000	3077.48	1859.79	1477.11	1301.73	1207.84	1153.37
155000	3180.06	1921.78	1526.35	1345.13	1248.10	1191.82
160000	3282.65	1983.77	1575.58	1388.52	1288.36	1230.26
165000	3385.23	2045.76	1624.82	1431.91	1328.62	1268.71
170000	3487.81	2107.76	1674.06	1475.30	1368.89	1307.15
175000	3590.39	2169.75	1723.29	1518.69	1409.15	1345.60
180000	3692.98	2231.74	1772.53	1562.08	1449.41	1384.04
185000	3795.56	2293.74	1821.77	1605.47	1489.67	1422.49
190000	3898.14	2355.73	1871.01	1648.86	1529.93	1460.94
195000	4000.72	2417.72	1920.24	1692.26	1570.19	1499.38
200000	4103.31	2479.71	1969.48	1735.65	1610.45	1537.83
205000	4205.89	2541.71	2018.72	1779.04	1650.72	1576.27
210000	4308.47	2603.70	2067.95	1822.43	1690.98	1614.72
215000	4411.05	2665.69	2117.19	1865.82	1731.24	1653.16
220000	4513.64	2727.69	2166.43	1909.21	1771.50	1691.61
225000	4616.22	2789.68	2215.66	1952.60	1811.76	1730.06
230000	4718.80	2851.67	2264.90	1995.99	1852.02	1768.50
235000	4821.38	2913.66	2314.14	2039.38	1892.28	1806.95
240000	4923.97	2975.66	2363.37	2082.78	1932.55	1845.39
245000	5026.55	3037.65	2412.61	2126.17	1972.81	1883.84
250000	5129.13	3099.64	2461.85	2169.56	2013.07	1922.28

Buying a Home When You're Single

Monthly Payments for
Interest: 9 %

Principal			Term (Years)			
	5	10	15	20	25	30
1000	20.76	12.67	10.14	9.00	8.39	8.05
5000	103.79	63.34	50.71	44.99	41.96	40.23
10000	207.58	126.68	101.43	89.97	83.92	80.46
15000	311.38	190.01	152.14	134.96	125.88	120.69
20000	415.17	253.35	202.85	179.95	167.84	160.92
25000	518.96	316.69	253.57	224.93	209.80	201.16
30000	622.75	380.03	304.28	269.92	251.76	241.39
35000	726.54	443.37	354.99	314.90	293.72	281.62
40000	830.33	506.70	405.71	359.89	335.68	321.85
45000	934.13	570.04	456.42	404.88	377.64	362.08
50000	1037.92	633.38	507.13	449.86	419.60	402.31
55000	1141.71	696.72	557.85	494.85	461.56	442.54
60000	1245.50	760.05	608.56	539.84	503.52	482.77
65000	1349.29	823.39	659.27	584.82	545.48	523.00
70000	1453.08	886.73	709.99	629.81	587.44	563.24
75000	1556.88	950.07	760.70	674.79	629.40	603.47
80000	1660.67	1013.41	811.41	719.78	671.36	643.70
85000	1764.46	1076.74	862.13	764.77	713.32	683.93
90000	1868.25	1140.08	912.84	809.75	755.28	724.16
95000	1972.04	1203.42	963.55	854.74	797.24	764.39
100000	2075.84	1266.76	1014.27	899.73	839.20	804.62
105000	2179.63	1330.10	1064.98	944.71	881.16	844.85
110000	2283.42	1393.43	1115.69	989.70	923.12	885.08
115000	2387.21	1456.77	1166.41	1034.68	965.08	925.32
120000	2491.00	1520.11	1217.12	1079.67	1007.04	965.55
125000	2594.79	1583.45	1267.83	1124.66	1049.00	1005.78
130000	2698.59	1646.79	1318.55	1169.64	1090.96	1046.01
135000	2802.38	1710.12	1369.26	1214.63	1132.92	1086.24
140000	2906.17	1773.46	1419.97	1259.62	1174.87	1126.47
145000	3009.96	1836.80	1470.69	1304.60	1216.83	1166.70
150000	3113.75	1900.14	1521.40	1349.59	1258.79	1206.93
155000	3217.55	1963.47	1572.11	1394.58	1300.75	1247.17
160000	3321.34	2026.81	1622.83	1439.56	1342.71	1287.40
165000	3425.13	2090.15	1673.54	1484.55	1384.67	1327.63
170000	3528.92	2153.49	1724.25	1529.53	1426.63	1367.86
175000	3632.71	2216.83	1774.97	1574.52	1468.59	1408.09
180000	3736.50	2280.16	1825.68	1619.51	1510.55	1448.32
185000	3840.30	2343.50	1876.39	1664.49	1552.51	1488.55
190000	3944.09	2406.84	1927.11	1709.48	1594.47	1528.78
195000	4047.88	2470.18	1977.82	1754.47	1636.43	1569.01
200000	4151.67	2533.52	2028.53	1799.45	1678.39	1609.25
205000	4255.46	2596.85	2079.25	1844.44	1720.35	1649.48
210000	4359.25	2660.19	2129.96	1889.42	1762.31	1689.71
215000	4463.05	2723.53	2180.67	1934.41	1804.27	1729.94
220000	4566.84	2786.87	2231.39	1979.40	1846.23	1770.17
225000	4670.63	2850.20	2282.10	2024.38	1888.19	1810.40
230000	4774.42	2913.54	2332.81	2069.37	1930.15	1850.63
235000	4878.21	2976.88	2383.53	2114.36	1972.11	1890.86
240000	4982.01	3040.22	2434.24	2159.34	2014.07	1931.09
245000	5085.80	3103.56	2484.95	2204.33	2056.03	1971.33
250000	5189.59	3166.89	2535.67	2249.31	2097.99	2011.56

Monthly Payments for
Interest: 9.5 %
Principal

Principal	5	10	Term (Years) 15	20	25	30
1000	21.00	12.94	10.44	9.32	8.74	8.41
5000	105.01	64.70	52.21	46.61	43.68	42.04
10000	210.02	129.40	104.42	93.21	87.37	84.09
15000	315.03	194.10	156.63	139.82	131.05	126.13
20000	420.04	258.80	208.84	186.43	174.74	168.17
25000	525.05	323.49	261.06	233.03	218.42	210.21
30000	630.06	388.19	313.27	279.64	262.11	252.26
35000	735.07	452.89	365.48	326.25	305.79	294.30
40000	840.07	517.59	417.69	372.85	349.48	336.34
45000	945.08	582.29	469.90	419.46	393.16	378.38
50000	1050.09	646.99	522.11	466.07	436.85	420.43
55000	1155.10	711.69	574.32	512.67	480.53	462.47
60000	1260.11	776.39	626.53	559.28	524.22	504.51
65000	1365.12	841.08	678.75	605.89	567.90	546.56
70000	1470.13	905.78	730.96	652.49	611.59	588.60
75000	1575.14	970.48	783.17	699.10	655.27	630.64
80000	1680.15	1035.18	835.38	745.70	698.96	672.68
85000	1785.16	1099.88	887.59	792.31	742.64	714.73
90000	1890.17	1164.58	939.80	838.92	786.33	756.77
95000	1995.18	1229.28	992.01	885.52	830.01	798.81
100000	2100.19	1293.98	1044.22	932.13	873.70	840.85
105000	2205.20	1358.67	1096.44	978.74	917.38	882.90
110000	2310.20	1423.37	1148.65	1025.34	961.07	924.94
115000	2415.21	1488.07	1200.86	1071.95	1004.75	966.98
120000	2520.22	1552.77	1253.07	1118.56	1048.44	1009.03
125000	2625.23	1617.47	1305.28	1165.16	1092.12	1051.07
130000	2730.24	1682.17	1357.49	1211.77	1135.81	1093.11
135000	2835.25	1746.87	1409.70	1258.38	1179.49	1135.15
140000	2940.26	1811.57	1461.91	1304.98	1223.18	1177.20
145000	3045.27	1876.26	1514.13	1351.59	1266.86	1219.24
150000	3150.28	1940.96	1566.34	1398.20	1310.54	1261.28
155000	3255.29	2005.66	1618.55	1444.80	1354.23	1303.32
160000	3360.30	2070.36	1670.76	1491.41	1397.91	1345.37
165000	3465.31	2135.06	1722.97	1538.02	1441.60	1387.41
170000	3570.32	2199.76	1775.18	1584.62	1485.28	1429.45
175000	3675.33	2264.46	1827.39	1631.23	1528.97	1471.49
180000	3780.34	2329.16	1879.60	1677.84	1572.65	1513.54
185000	3885.34	2393.85	1931.82	1724.44	1616.34	1555.58
190000	3990.35	2458.55	1984.03	1771.05	1660.02	1597.62
195000	4095.36	2523.25	2036.24	1817.66	1703.71	1639.67
200000	4200.37	2587.95	2088.45	1864.26	1747.39	1681.71
205000	4305.38	2652.65	2140.66	1910.87	1791.08	1723.75
210000	4410.39	2717.35	2192.87	1957.48	1834.76	1765.79
215000	4515.40	2782.05	2245.08	2004.08	1878.45	1807.84
220000	4620.41	2846.75	2297.29	2050.69	1922.13	1849.88
225000	4725.42	2911.45	2349.51	2097.30	1965.82	1891.92
230000	4830.43	2976.14	2401.72	2143.90	2009.50	1933.96
235000	4935.44	3040.84	2453.93	2190.51	2053.19	1976.01
240000	5040.45	3105.54	2506.14	2237.11	2096.87	2018.05
245000	5145.46	3170.24	2558.35	2283.72	2140.56	2060.09
250000	5250.47	3234.94	2610.56	2330.33	2184.24	2102.14

Buying a Home When You're Single

Monthly Payments for
Interest: 10 %
Term (Years)

Principal	5	10	15	20	25	30
1000	21.25	13.22	10.75	9.65	9.09	8.78
5000	106.24	66.08	53.73	48.25	45.44	43.88
10000	212.47	132.15	107.46	96.50	90.87	87.76
15000	318.71	198.23	161.19	144.75	136.31	131.64
20000	424.94	264.30	214.92	193.00	181.74	175.51
25000	531.18	330.38	268.65	241.26	227.18	219.39
30000	637.41	396.45	322.38	289.51	272.61	263.27
35000	743.65	462.53	376.11	337.76	318.05	307.15
40000	849.88	528.60	429.84	386.01	363.48	351.03
45000	956.12	594.68	483.57	434.26	408.92	394.91
50000	1062.35	660.75	537.30	482.51	454.35	438.79
55000	1168.59	726.83	591.03	530.76	499.79	482.66
60000	1274.82	792.90	644.76	579.01	545.22	526.54
65000	1381.06	858.98	698.49	627.26	590.66	570.42
70000	1487.29	925.06	752.22	675.52	636.09	614.30
75000	1593.53	991.13	805.95	723.77	681.53	658.18
80000	1699.76	1057.21	859.68	772.02	726.96	702.06
85000	1806.00	1123.28	913.41	820.27	772.40	745.94
90000	1912.23	1189.36	967.14	868.52	817.83	789.81
95000	2018.47	1255.43	1020.87	916.77	863.27	833.69
100000	2124.70	1321.51	1074.61	965.02	908.70	877.57
105000	2230.94	1387.58	1128.34	1013.27	954.14	921.45
110000	2337.17	1453.66	1182.07	1061.52	999.57	965.33
115000	2443.41	1519.73	1235.80	1109.77	1045.01	1009.21
120000	2549.65	1585.81	1289.53	1158.03	1090.44	1053.09
125000	2655.88	1651.88	1343.26	1206.28	1135.88	1096.96
130000	2762.12	1717.96	1396.99	1254.53	1181.31	1140.84
135000	2868.35	1784.03	1450.72	1302.78	1226.75	1184.72
140000	2974.59	1850.11	1504.45	1351.03	1272.18	1228.60
145000	3080.82	1916.19	1558.18	1399.28	1317.62	1272.48
150000	3187.06	1982.26	1611.91	1447.53	1363.05	1316.36
155000	3293.29	2048.34	1665.64	1495.78	1408.49	1360.24
160000	3399.53	2114.41	1719.37	1544.03	1453.92	1404.11
165000	3505.76	2180.49	1773.10	1592.29	1499.36	1447.99
170000	3612.00	2246.56	1826.83	1640.54	1544.79	1491.87
175000	3718.23	2312.64	1880.56	1688.79	1590.23	1535.75
180000	3824.47	2378.71	1934.29	1737.04	1635.66	1579.63
185000	3930.70	2444.79	1988.02	1785.29	1681.10	1623.51
190000	4036.94	2510.86	2041.75	1833.54	1726.53	1667.39
195000	4143.17	2576.94	2095.48	1881.79	1771.97	1711.26
200000	4249.41	2643.01	2149.21	1930.04	1817.40	1755.14
205000	4355.64	2709.09	2202.94	1978.29	1862.84	1799.02
210000	4461.88	2775.17	2256.67	2026.55	1908.27	1842.90
215000	4568.11	2841.24	2310.40	2074.80	1953.71	1886.78
220000	4674.35	2907.32	2364.13	2123.05	1999.14	1930.66
225000	4780.59	2973.39	2417.86	2171.30	2044.58	1974.54
230000	4886.82	3039.47	2471.59	2219.55	2090.01	2018.41
235000	4993.06	3105.54	2525.32	2267.80	2135.45	2062.29
240000	5099.29	3171.62	2579.05	2316.05	2180.88	2106.17
245000	5205.53	3237.69	2632.78	2364.30	2226.32	2150.05
250000	5311.76	3303.77	2686.51	2412.55	2271.75	2193.93

Appendix II — Amortization Tables

Monthly Payments for
Interest: 10.5 %

Principal	5	10	Term (Years) 15	20	25	30
1000	21.49	13.49	11.05	9.98	9.44	9.15
5000	107.47	67.47	55.27	49.92	47.21	45.74
10000	214.94	134.93	110.54	99.84	94.42	91.47
15000	322.41	202.40	165.81	149.76	141.63	137.21
20000	429.88	269.87	221.08	199.68	188.84	182.95
25000	537.35	337.34	276.35	249.59	236.05	228.68
30000	644.82	404.80	331.62	299.51	283.25	274.42
35000	752.29	472.27	386.89	349.43	330.46	320.16
40000	859.76	539.74	442.16	399.35	377.67	365.90
45000	967.23	607.21	497.43	449.27	424.88	411.63
50000	1074.70	674.67	552.70	499.19	472.09	457.37
55000	1182.16	742.14	607.97	549.11	519.30	503.11
60000	1289.63	809.61	663.24	599.03	566.51	548.84
65000	1397.10	877.08	718.51	648.95	613.72	594.58
70000	1504.57	944.54	773.78	698.87	660.93	640.32
75000	1612.04	1012.01	829.05	748.78	708.14	686.05
80000	1719.51	1079.48	884.32	798.70	755.35	731.79
85000	1826.98	1146.95	939.59	848.62	802.55	777.53
90000	1934.45	1214.41	994.86	898.54	849.76	823.27
95000	2041.92	1281.88	1050.13	948.46	896.97	869.00
100000	2149.39	1349.35	1105.40	998.38	944.18	914.74
105000	2256.86	1416.82	1160.67	1048.30	991.39	960.48
110000	2364.33	1484.28	1215.94	1098.22	1038.60	1006.21
115000	2471.80	1551.75	1271.21	1148.14	1085.81	1051.95
120000	2579.27	1619.22	1326.48	1198.06	1133.02	1097.69
125000	2686.74	1686.69	1381.75	1247.97	1180.23	1143.42
130000	2794.21	1754.15	1437.02	1297.89	1227.44	1189.16
135000	2901.68	1821.62	1492.29	1347.81	1274.65	1234.90
140000	3009.15	1889.09	1547.56	1397.73	1321.85	1280.64
145000	3116.62	1956.56	1602.83	1447.65	1369.06	1326.37
150000	3224.09	2024.02	1658.10	1497.57	1416.27	1372.11
155000	3331.55	2091.49	1713.37	1547.49	1463.48	1417.85
160000	3439.02	2158.96	1768.64	1597.41	1510.69	1463.58
165000	3546.49	2226.43	1823.91	1647.33	1557.90	1509.32
170000	3653.96	2293.89	1879.18	1697.25	1605.11	1555.06
175000	3761.43	2361.36	1934.45	1747.16	1652.32	1600.79
180000	3868.90	2428.83	1989.72	1797.08	1699.53	1646.53
185000	3976.37	2496.30	2044.99	1847.00	1746.74	1692.27
190000	4083.84	2563.76	2100.26	1896.92	1793.95	1738.00
195000	4191.31	2631.23	2155.53	1946.84	1841.15	1783.74
200000	4298.78	2698.70	2210.80	1996.76	1888.36	1829.48
205000	4406.25	2766.17	2266.07	2046.68	1935.57	1875.22
210000	4513.72	2833.63	2321.34	2096.60	1982.78	1920.95
215000	4621.19	2901.10	2376.61	2146.52	2029.99	1966.69
220000	4728.66	2968.57	2431.88	2196.44	2077.20	2012.43
225000	4836.13	3036.04	2487.15	2246.35	2124.41	2058.16
230000	4943.60	3103.50	2542.42	2296.27	2171.62	2103.90
235000	5051.07	3170.97	2597.69	2346.19	2218.83	2149.64
240000	5158.54	3238.44	2652.96	2396.11	2266.04	2195.37
245000	5266.01	3305.91	2708.23	2446.03	2313.25	2241.11
250000	5373.48	3373.37	2763.50	2495.95	2360.45	2286.85

179

Buying a Home When You're Single

Monthly Payments for
Interest: 11 %
Term (Years)

Principal	5	10	15	20	25	30
1000	21.74	13.78	11.37	10.32	9.80	9.52
5000	108.71	68.88	56.83	51.61	49.01	47.62
10000	217.42	137.75	113.66	103.22	98.01	95.23
15000	326.14	206.63	170.49	154.83	147.02	142.85
20000	434.85	275.50	227.32	206.44	196.02	190.46
25000	543.56	344.38	284.15	258.05	245.03	238.08
30000	652.27	413.25	340.98	309.66	294.03	285.70
35000	760.98	482.13	397.81	361.27	343.04	333.31
40000	869.70	551.00	454.64	412.88	392.05	380.93
45000	978.41	619.88	511.47	464.48	441.05	428.55
50000	1087.12	688.75	568.30	516.09	490.06	476.16
55000	1195.83	757.63	625.13	567.70	539.06	523.78
60000	1304.55	826.50	681.96	619.31	588.07	571.39
65000	1413.26	895.38	738.79	670.92	637.07	619.01
70000	1521.97	964.25	795.62	722.53	686.08	666.63
75000	1630.68	1033.13	852.45	774.14	735.08	714.24
80000	1739.39	1102.00	909.28	825.75	784.09	761.86
85000	1848.11	1170.88	966.11	877.36	833.10	809.47
90000	1956.82	1239.75	1022.94	928.97	882.10	857.09
95000	2065.53	1308.63	1079.77	980.58	931.11	904.71
100000	2174.24	1377.50	1136.60	1032.19	980.11	952.32
105000	2282.95	1446.38	1193.43	1083.80	1029.12	999.94
110000	2391.67	1515.25	1250.26	1135.41	1078.12	1047.56
115000	2500.38	1584.13	1307.09	1187.02	1127.13	1095.17
120000	2609.09	1653.00	1363.92	1238.63	1176.14	1142.79
125000	2717.80	1721.88	1420.75	1290.24	1225.14	1190.40
130000	2826.51	1790.75	1477.58	1341.84	1274.15	1238.02
135000	2935.23	1859.63	1534.41	1393.45	1323.15	1285.64
140000	3043.94	1928.50	1591.24	1445.06	1372.16	1333.25
145000	3152.65	1997.38	1648.07	1496.67	1421.16	1380.87
150000	3261.36	2066.25	1704.90	1548.28	1470.17	1428.49
155000	3370.08	2135.13	1761.73	1599.89	1519.18	1476.10
160000	3478.79	2204.00	1818.56	1651.50	1568.18	1523.72
165000	3587.50	2272.88	1875.38	1703.11	1617.19	1571.33
170000	3696.21	2341.75	1932.21	1754.72	1666.19	1618.95
175000	3804.92	2410.63	1989.04	1806.33	1715.20	1666.57
180000	3913.64	2479.50	2045.87	1857.94	1764.20	1714.18
185000	4022.35	2548.38	2102.70	1909.55	1813.21	1761.80
190000	4131.06	2617.25	2159.53	1961.16	1862.21	1809.41
195000	4239.77	2686.13	2216.36	2012.77	1911.22	1857.03
200000	4348.48	2755.00	2273.19	2064.38	1960.23	1904.65
205000	4457.20	2823.88	2330.02	2115.99	2009.23	1952.26
210000	4565.91	2892.75	2386.85	2167.60	2058.24	1999.88
215000	4674.62	2961.63	2443.68	2219.21	2107.24	2047.50
220000	4783.33	3030.50	2500.51	2270.81	2156.25	2095.11
225000	4892.05	3099.38	2557.34	2322.42	2205.25	2142.73
230000	5000.76	3168.25	2614.17	2374.03	2254.26	2190.34
235000	5109.47	3237.13	2671.00	2425.64	2303.27	2237.96
240000	5218.18	3306.00	2727.83	2477.25	2352.27	2285.58
245000	5326.89	3374.88	2784.66	2528.86	2401.28	2333.19
250000	5435.61	3443.75	2841.49	2580.47	2450.28	2380.81

Appendix II — Amortization Tables

Monthly Payments for
Interest: 11.5 %

Principal	5	10	15	20	25	30
1000	21.99	14.06	11.68	10.66	10.16	9.90
5000	109.96	70.30	58.41	53.32	50.82	49.51
10000	219.93	140.60	116.82	106.64	101.65	99.03
15000	329.89	210.89	175.23	159.96	152.47	148.54
20000	439.85	281.19	233.64	213.29	203.29	198.06
25000	549.82	351.49	292.05	266.61	254.12	247.57
30000	659.78	421.79	350.46	319.93	304.94	297.09
35000	769.74	492.08	408.87	373.25	355.76	346.60
40000	879.70	562.38	467.28	426.57	406.59	396.12
45000	989.67	632.68	525.69	479.89	457.41	445.63
50000	1099.63	702.98	584.09	533.21	508.23	495.15
55000	1209.59	773.27	642.50	586.54	559.06	544.66
60000	1319.56	843.57	700.91	639.86	609.88	594.17
65000	1429.52	913.87	759.32	693.18	660.70	643.69
70000	1539.48	984.17	817.73	746.50	711.53	693.20
75000	1649.45	1054.47	876.14	799.82	762.35	742.72
80000	1759.41	1124.76	934.55	853.14	813.18	792.23
85000	1869.37	1195.06	992.96	906.47	864.00	841.75
90000	1979.33	1265.36	1051.37	959.79	914.82	891.26
95000	2089.30	1335.66	1109.78	1013.11	965.65	940.78
100000	2199.26	1405.95	1168.19	1066.43	1016.47	990.29
105000	2309.22	1476.25	1226.60	1119.75	1067.29	1039.81
110000	2419.19	1546.55	1285.01	1173.07	1118.12	1089.32
115000	2529.15	1616.85	1343.42	1226.39	1168.94	1138.84
120000	2639.11	1687.15	1401.83	1279.72	1219.76	1188.35
125000	2749.08	1757.44	1460.24	1333.04	1270.59	1237.86
130000	2859.04	1827.74	1518.65	1386.36	1321.41	1287.38
135000	2969.00	1898.04	1577.06	1439.68	1372.23	1336.89
140000	3078.97	1968.34	1635.47	1493.00	1423.06	1386.41
145000	3188.93	2038.63	1693.88	1546.32	1473.88	1435.92
150000	3298.89	2108.93	1752.28	1599.64	1524.70	1485.44
155000	3408.85	2179.23	1810.69	1652.97	1575.53	1534.95
160000	3518.82	2249.53	1869.10	1706.29	1626.35	1584.47
165000	3628.78	2319.82	1927.51	1759.61	1677.17	1633.98
170000	3738.74	2390.12	1985.92	1812.93	1728.00	1683.50
175000	3848.71	2460.42	2044.33	1866.25	1778.82	1733.01
180000	3958.67	2530.72	2102.74	1919.57	1829.64	1782.52
185000	4068.63	2601.02	2161.15	1972.89	1880.47	1832.04
190000	4178.60	2671.31	2219.56	2026.22	1931.29	1881.55
195000	4288.56	2741.61	2277.97	2079.54	1982.11	1931.07
200000	4398.52	2811.91	2336.38	2132.86	2032.94	1980.58
205000	4508.48	2882.21	2394.79	2186.18	2083.76	2030.10
210000	4618.45	2952.50	2453.20	2239.50	2134.58	2079.61
215000	4728.41	3022.80	2511.61	2292.82	2185.41	2129.13
220000	4838.37	3093.10	2570.02	2346.15	2236.23	2178.64
225000	4948.34	3163.40	2628.43	2399.47	2287.06	2228.16
230000	5058.30	3233.70	2686.84	2452.79	2337.88	2277.67
235000	5168.26	3303.99	2745.25	2506.11	2388.70	2327.18
240000	5278.23	3374.29	2803.66	2559.43	2439.53	2376.70
245000	5388.19	3444.59	2862.07	2612.75	2490.35	2426.21
250000	5498.15	3514.89	2920.47	2666.07	2541.17	2475.73

Buying a Home When You're Single

Monthly Payments for
Interest: 12 %

Term (Years)

Principal	5	10	15	20	25	30
1000	22.24	14.35	12.00	11.01	10.53	10.29
5000	111.22	71.74	60.01	55.05	52.66	51.43
10000	222.44	143.47	120.02	110.11	105.32	102.86
15000	333.67	215.21	180.03	165.16	157.98	154.29
20000	444.89	286.94	240.03	220.22	210.64	205.72
25000	556.11	358.68	300.04	275.27	263.31	257.15
30000	667.33	430.41	360.05	330.33	315.97	308.58
35000	778.56	502.15	420.06	385.38	368.63	360.01
40000	889.78	573.88	480.07	440.43	421.29	411.45
45000	1001.00	645.62	540.08	495.49	473.95	462.88
50000	1112.22	717.35	600.08	550.54	526.61	514.31
55000	1223.44	789.09	660.09	605.60	579.27	565.74
60000	1334.67	860.83	720.10	660.65	631.93	617.17
65000	1445.89	932.56	780.11	715.71	684.60	668.60
70000	1557.11	1004.30	840.12	770.76	737.26	720.03
75000	1668.33	1076.03	900.13	825.81	789.92	771.46
80000	1779.56	1147.77	960.13	880.87	842.58	822.89
85000	1890.78	1219.50	1020.14	935.92	895.24	874.32
90000	2002.00	1291.24	1080.15	990.98	947.90	925.75
95000	2113.22	1362.97	1140.16	1046.03	1000.56	977.18
100000	2224.44	1434.71	1200.17	1101.09	1053.22	1028.61
105000	2335.67	1506.44	1260.18	1156.14	1105.89	1080.04
110000	2446.89	1578.18	1320.18	1211.19	1158.55	1131.47
115000	2558.11	1649.92	1380.19	1266.25	1211.21	1182.90
120000	2669.33	1721.65	1440.20	1321.30	1263.87	1234.34
125000	2780.56	1793.39	1500.21	1376.36	1316.53	1285.77
130000	2891.78	1865.12	1560.22	1431.41	1369.19	1337.20
135000	3003.00	1936.86	1620.23	1486.47	1421.85	1388.63
140000	3114.22	2008.59	1680.24	1541.52	1474.51	1440.06
145000	3225.44	2080.33	1740.24	1596.57	1527.18	1491.49
150000	3336.67	2152.06	1800.25	1651.63	1579.84	1542.92
155000	3447.89	2223.80	1860.26	1706.68	1632.50	1594.35
160000	3559.11	2295.54	1920.27	1761.74	1685.16	1645.78
165000	3670.33	2367.27	1980.28	1816.79	1737.82	1697.21
170000	3781.56	2439.01	2040.29	1871.85	1790.48	1748.64
175000	3892.78	2510.74	2100.29	1926.90	1843.14	1800.07
180000	4004.00	2582.48	2160.30	1981.96	1895.80	1851.50
185000	4115.22	2654.21	2220.31	2037.01	1948.46	1902.93
190000	4226.45	2725.95	2280.32	2092.06	2001.13	1954.36
195000	4337.67	2797.68	2340.33	2147.12	2053.79	2005.79
200000	4448.89	2869.42	2400.34	2202.17	2106.45	2057.23
205000	4560.11	2941.15	2460.34	2257.23	2159.11	2108.66
210000	4671.33	3012.89	2520.35	2312.28	2211.77	2160.09
215000	4782.56	3084.63	2580.36	2367.34	2264.43	2211.52
220000	4893.78	3156.36	2640.37	2422.39	2317.09	2262.95
225000	5005.00	3228.10	2700.38	2477.44	2369.75	2314.38
230000	5116.22	3299.83	2760.39	2532.50	2422.42	2365.81
235000	5227.45	3371.57	2820.39	2587.55	2475.08	2417.24
240000	5338.67	3443.30	2880.40	2642.61	2527.74	2468.67
245000	5449.89	3515.04	2940.41	2697.66	2580.40	2520.10
250000	5561.11	3586.77	3000.42	2752.72	2633.06	2571.53

Monthly Payments for
Interest: 12.5 %   Term (Years)

Principal	5	10	15	20	25	30
1000	22.50	14.64	12.33	11.36	10.90	10.67
5000	112.49	73.19	61.63	56.81	54.52	53.36
10000	224.98	146.38	123.25	113.61	109.04	106.73
15000	337.47	219.56	184.88	170.42	163.55	160.09
20000	449.96	292.75	246.50	227.23	218.07	213.45
25000	562.45	365.94	308.13	284.04	272.59	266.81
30000	674.94	439.13	369.76	340.84	327.11	320.18
35000	787.43	512.32	431.38	397.65	381.62	373.54
40000	899.92	585.50	493.01	454.46	436.14	426.90
45000	1012.41	658.69	554.63	511.26	490.66	480.27
50000	1124.90	731.88	616.26	568.07	545.18	533.63
55000	1237.39	805.07	677.89	624.88	599.69	586.99
60000	1349.88	878.26	739.51	681.68	654.21	640.35
65000	1462.37	951.45	801.14	738.49	708.73	693.72
70000	1574.86	1024.63	862.77	795.30	763.25	747.08
75000	1687.35	1097.82	924.39	852.11	817.77	800.44
80000	1799.84	1171.01	986.02	908.91	872.28	853.81
85000	1912.32	1244.20	1047.64	965.72	926.80	907.17
90000	2024.81	1317.39	1109.27	1022.53	981.32	960.53
95000	2137.30	1390.57	1170.90	1079.33	1035.84	1013.89
100000	2249.79	1463.76	1232.52	1136.14	1090.35	1067.26
105000	2362.28	1536.95	1294.15	1192.95	1144.87	1120.62
110000	2474.77	1610.14	1355.77	1249.75	1199.39	1173.98
115000	2587.26	1683.33	1417.40	1306.56	1253.91	1227.35
120000	2699.75	1756.51	1479.03	1363.37	1308.42	1280.71
125000	2812.24	1829.70	1540.65	1420.18	1362.94	1334.07
130000	2924.73	1902.89	1602.28	1476.98	1417.46	1387.44
135000	3037.22	1976.08	1663.90	1533.79	1471.98	1440.80
140000	3149.71	2049.27	1725.53	1590.60	1526.50	1494.16
145000	3262.20	2122.45	1787.16	1647.40	1581.01	1547.52
150000	3374.69	2195.64	1848.78	1704.21	1635.53	1600.89
155000	3487.18	2268.83	1910.41	1761.02	1690.05	1654.25
160000	3599.67	2342.02	1972.04	1817.82	1744.57	1707.61
165000	3712.16	2415.21	2033.66	1874.63	1799.08	1760.98
170000	3824.65	2488.39	2095.29	1931.44	1853.60	1814.34
175000	3937.14	2561.58	2156.91	1988.25	1908.12	1867.70
180000	4049.63	2634.77	2218.54	2045.05	1962.64	1921.06
185000	4162.12	2707.96	2280.17	2101.86	2017.16	1974.43
190000	4274.61	2781.15	2341.79	2158.67	2071.67	2027.79
195000	4387.10	2854.34	2403.42	2215.47	2126.19	2081.15
200000	4499.59	2927.52	2465.04	2272.28	2180.71	2134.52
205000	4612.08	3000.71	2526.67	2329.09	2235.23	2187.88
210000	4724.57	3073.90	2588.30	2385.90	2289.74	2241.24
215000	4837.06	3147.09	2649.92	2442.70	2344.26	2294.60
220000	4949.55	3220.28	2711.55	2499.51	2398.78	2347.97
225000	5062.04	3293.46	2773.17	2556.32	2453.30	2401.33
230000	5174.53	3366.65	2834.80	2613.12	2507.81	2454.69
235000	5287.02	3439.84	2896.43	2669.93	2562.33	2508.06
240000	5399.51	3513.03	2958.05	2726.74	2616.85	2561.42
245000	5511.99	3586.22	3019.68	2783.54	2671.37	2614.78
250000	5624.48	3659.40	3081.31	2840.35	2725.89	2668.14

Monthly Payments for
Interest: 13 %

Principal	5	10	Term (Years) 15	20	25	30
1000	22.75	14.93	12.65	11.72	11.28	11.06
5000	113.77	74.66	63.26	58.58	56.39	55.31
10000	227.53	149.31	126.52	117.16	112.78	110.62
15000	341.30	223.97	189.79	175.74	169.18	165.93
20000	455.06	298.62	253.05	234.32	225.57	221.24
25000	568.83	373.28	316.31	292.89	281.96	276.55
30000	682.59	447.93	379.57	351.47	338.35	331.86
35000	796.36	522.59	442.83	410.05	394.74	387.17
40000	910.12	597.24	506.10	468.63	451.13	442.48
45000	1023.89	671.90	569.36	527.21	507.53	497.79
50000	1137.65	746.55	632.62	585.79	563.92	553.10
55000	1251.42	821.21	695.88	644.37	620.31	608.41
60000	1365.18	895.86	759.15	702.95	676.70	663.72
65000	1478.95	970.52	822.41	761.52	733.09	719.03
70000	1592.72	1045.18	885.67	820.10	789.48	774.34
75000	1706.48	1119.83	948.93	878.68	845.88	829.65
80000	1820.25	1194.49	1012.19	937.26	902.27	884.96
85000	1934.01	1269.14	1075.46	995.84	958.66	940.27
90000	2047.78	1343.80	1138.72	1054.42	1015.05	995.58
95000	2161.54	1418.45	1201.98	1113.00	1071.44	1050.89
100000	2275.31	1493.11	1265.24	1171.58	1127.84	1106.20
105000	2389.07	1567.76	1328.50	1230.15	1184.23	1161.51
110000	2502.84	1642.42	1391.77	1288.73	1240.62	1216.82
115000	2616.60	1717.07	1455.03	1347.31	1297.01	1272.13
120000	2730.37	1791.73	1518.29	1405.89	1353.40	1327.44
125000	2844.13	1866.38	1581.55	1464.47	1409.79	1382.75
130000	2957.90	1941.04	1644.81	1523.05	1466.19	1438.06
135000	3071.66	2015.69	1708.08	1581.63	1522.58	1493.37
140000	3185.43	2090.35	1771.34	1640.21	1578.97	1548.68
145000	3299.20	2165.01	1834.60	1698.78	1635.36	1603.99
150000	3412.96	2239.66	1897.86	1757.36	1691.75	1659.30
155000	3526.73	2314.32	1961.13	1815.94	1748.14	1714.61
160000	3640.49	2388.97	2024.39	1874.52	1804.54	1769.92
165000	3754.26	2463.63	2087.65	1933.10	1860.93	1825.23
170000	3868.02	2538.28	2150.91	1991.68	1917.32	1880.54
175000	3981.79	2612.94	2214.17	2050.26	1973.71	1935.85
180000	4095.55	2687.59	2277.44	2108.84	2030.10	1991.16
185000	4209.32	2762.25	2340.70	2167.42	2086.50	2046.47
190000	4323.08	2836.90	2403.96	2225.99	2142.89	2101.78
195000	4436.85	2911.56	2467.22	2284.57	2199.28	2157.09
200000	4550.61	2986.21	2530.48	2343.15	2255.67	2212.40
205000	4664.38	3060.87	2593.75	2401.73	2312.06	2267.71
210000	4778.15	3135.53	2657.01	2460.31	2368.45	2323.02
215000	4891.91	3210.18	2720.27	2518.89	2424.85	2378.33
220000	5005.68	3284.84	2783.53	2577.47	2481.24	2433.64
225000	5119.44	3359.49	2846.79	2636.05	2537.63	2488.95
230000	5233.21	3434.15	2910.06	2694.62	2594.02	2544.26
235000	5346.97	3508.80	2973.32	2753.20	2650.41	2599.57
240000	5460.74	3583.46	3036.58	2811.78	2706.80	2654.88
245000	5574.50	3658.11	3099.84	2870.36	2763.20	2710.19
250000	5688.27	3732.77	3163.11	2928.94	2819.59	2765.50

Monthly Payments for
Interest: 13.5 %   Term (Years)

Principal	5	10	15	20	25	30
1000	23.01	15.23	12.98	12.07	11.66	11.45
5000	115.05	76.14	64.92	60.37	58.28	57.27
10000	230.10	152.27	129.83	120.74	116.56	114.54
15000	345.15	228.41	194.75	181.11	174.85	171.81
20000	460.20	304.55	259.66	241.47	233.13	229.08
25000	575.25	380.69	324.58	301.84	291.41	286.35
30000	690.30	456.82	389.50	362.21	349.69	343.62
35000	805.34	532.96	454.41	422.58	407.98	400.89
40000	920.39	609.10	519.33	482.95	466.26	458.16
45000	1035.44	685.23	584.24	543.32	524.54	515.44
50000	1150.49	761.37	649.16	603.69	582.82	572.71
55000	1265.54	837.51	714.08	664.06	641.10	629.98
60000	1380.59	913.65	778.99	724.42	699.39	687.25
65000	1495.64	989.78	843.91	784.79	757.67	744.52
70000	1610.69	1065.92	908.82	845.16	815.95	801.79
75000	1725.74	1142.06	973.74	905.53	874.23	859.06
80000	1840.79	1218.19	1038.65	965.90	932.52	916.33
85000	1955.84	1294.33	1103.57	1026.27	990.80	973.60
90000	2070.89	1370.47	1168.49	1086.64	1049.08	1030.87
95000	2185.94	1446.61	1233.40	1147.01	1107.36	1088.14
100000	2300.98	1522.74	1298.32	1207.37	1165.64	1145.41
105000	2416.03	1598.88	1363.23	1267.74	1223.93	1202.68
110000	2531.08	1675.02	1428.15	1328.11	1282.21	1259.95
115000	2646.13	1751.15	1493.07	1388.48	1340.49	1317.22
120000	2761.18	1827.29	1557.98	1448.85	1398.77	1374.49
125000	2876.23	1903.43	1622.90	1509.22	1457.06	1431.77
130000	2991.28	1979.57	1687.81	1569.59	1515.34	1489.04
135000	3106.33	2055.70	1752.73	1629.96	1573.62	1546.31
140000	3221.38	2131.84	1817.65	1690.32	1631.90	1603.58
145000	3336.43	2207.98	1882.56	1750.69	1690.19	1660.85
150000	3451.48	2284.11	1947.48	1811.06	1748.47	1718.12
155000	3566.53	2360.25	2012.39	1871.43	1806.75	1775.39
160000	3681.58	2436.39	2077.31	1931.80	1865.03	1832.66
165000	3796.62	2512.53	2142.23	1992.17	1923.31	1889.93
170000	3911.67	2588.66	2207.14	2052.54	1981.60	1947.20
175000	4026.72	2664.80	2272.06	2112.91	2039.88	2004.47
180000	4141.77	2740.94	2336.97	2173.27	2098.16	2061.74
185000	4256.82	2817.07	2401.89	2233.64	2156.44	2119.01
190000	4371.87	2893.21	2466.81	2294.01	2214.73	2176.28
195000	4486.92	2969.35	2531.72	2354.38	2273.01	2233.55
200000	4601.97	3045.49	2596.64	2414.75	2331.29	2290.82
205000	4717.02	3121.62	2661.55	2475.12	2389.57	2348.09
210000	4832.07	3197.76	2726.47	2535.49	2447.85	2405.37
215000	4947.12	3273.90	2791.38	2595.86	2506.14	2462.64
220000	5062.17	3350.03	2856.30	2656.22	2564.42	2519.91
225000	5177.22	3426.17	2921.22	2716.59	2622.70	2577.18
230000	5292.26	3502.31	2986.13	2776.96	2680.98	2634.45
235000	5407.31	3578.45	3051.05	2837.33	2739.27	2691.72
240000	5522.36	3654.58	3115.96	2897.70	2797.55	2748.99
245000	5637.41	3730.72	3180.88	2958.07	2855.83	2806.26
250000	5752.46	3806.86	3245.80	3018.44	2914.11	2863.53

Buying a Home When You're Single

Monthly Payments for
Interest: 14 %

Principal	5	10	Term (Years) 15	20	25	30
1000	23.27	15.53	13.32	12.44	12.04	11.85
5000	116.34	77.63	66.59	62.18	60.19	59.24
10000	232.68	155.27	133.17	124.35	120.38	118.49
15000	349.02	232.90	199.76	186.53	180.56	177.73
20000	465.37	310.53	266.35	248.70	240.75	236.97
25000	581.71	388.17	332.94	310.88	300.94	296.22
30000	698.05	465.80	399.52	373.06	361.13	355.46
35000	814.39	543.43	466.11	435.23	421.32	414.71
40000	930.73	621.07	532.70	497.41	481.50	473.95
45000	1047.07	698.70	599.28	559.58	541.69	533.19
50000	1163.41	776.33	665.87	621.76	601.88	592.44
55000	1279.75	853.97	732.46	683.94	662.07	651.68
60000	1396.10	931.60	799.04	746.11	722.26	710.92
65000	1512.44	1009.23	865.63	808.29	782.44	770.17
70000	1628.78	1086.87	932.22	870.46	842.63	829.41
75000	1745.12	1164.50	998.81	932.64	902.82	888.65
80000	1861.46	1242.13	1065.39	994.82	963.01	947.90
85000	1977.80	1319.76	1131.98	1056.99	1023.20	1007.14
90000	2094.14	1397.40	1198.57	1119.17	1083.38	1066.38
95000	2210.48	1475.03	1265.15	1181.34	1143.57	1125.63
100000	2326.83	1552.66	1331.74	1243.52	1203.76	1184.87
105000	2443.17	1630.30	1398.33	1305.70	1263.95	1244.12
110000	2559.51	1707.93	1464.92	1367.87	1324.14	1303.36
115000	2675.85	1785.56	1531.50	1430.05	1384.33	1362.60
120000	2792.19	1863.20	1598.09	1492.22	1444.51	1421.85
125000	2908.53	1940.83	1664.68	1554.40	1504.70	1481.09
130000	3024.87	2018.46	1731.26	1616.58	1564.89	1540.33
135000	3141.21	2096.10	1797.85	1678.75	1625.08	1599.58
140000	3257.56	2173.73	1864.44	1740.93	1685.27	1658.82
145000	3373.90	2251.36	1931.03	1803.11	1745.45	1718.06
150000	3490.24	2329.00	1997.61	1865.28	1805.64	1777.31
155000	3606.58	2406.63	2064.20	1927.46	1865.83	1836.55
160000	3722.92	2484.26	2130.79	1989.63	1926.02	1895.79
165000	3839.26	2561.90	2197.37	2051.81	1986.21	1955.04
170000	3955.60	2639.53	2263.96	2113.99	2046.39	2014.28
175000	4071.94	2717.16	2330.55	2176.16	2106.58	2073.53
180000	4188.29	2794.80	2397.13	2238.34	2166.77	2132.77
185000	4304.63	2872.43	2463.72	2300.51	2226.96	2192.01
190000	4420.97	2950.06	2530.31	2362.69	2287.15	2251.26
195000	4537.31	3027.70	2596.90	2424.87	2347.33	2310.50
200000	4653.65	3105.33	2663.48	2487.04	2407.52	2369.74
205000	4769.99	3182.96	2730.07	2549.22	2467.71	2428.99
210000	4886.33	3260.60	2796.66	2611.39	2527.90	2488.23
215000	5002.67	3338.23	2863.24	2673.57	2588.09	2547.47
220000	5119.02	3415.86	2929.83	2735.75	2648.27	2606.72
225000	5235.36	3493.49	2996.42	2797.92	2708.46	2665.96
230000	5351.70	3571.13	3063.01	2860.10	2768.65	2725.21
235000	5468.04	3648.76	3129.59	2922.27	2828.84	2784.45
240000	5584.38	3726.39	3196.18	2984.45	2889.03	2843.69
245000	5700.72	3804.03	3262.77	3046.63	2949.21	2902.94
250000	5817.06	3881.66	3329.35	3108.80	3009.40	2962.18

186

Monthly Payments for
Interest: 14.5 %   Term (Years)

Principal	5	10	15	20	25	30
1000	23.53	15.83	13.66	12.80	12.42	12.25
5000	117.64	79.14	68.28	64.00	62.11	61.23
10000	235.28	158.29	136.55	128.00	124.22	122.46
15000	352.92	237.43	204.83	192.00	186.32	183.68
20000	470.57	316.57	273.10	256.00	248.43	244.91
25000	588.21	395.72	341.38	320.00	310.54	306.14
30000	705.85	474.86	409.65	384.00	372.65	367.37
35000	823.49	554.00	477.93	448.00	434.76	428.59
40000	941.13	633.15	546.20	512.00	496.87	489.82
45000	1058.77	712.29	614.48	576.00	558.97	551.05
50000	1176.41	791.43	682.75	640.00	621.08	612.28
55000	1294.06	870.58	751.03	704.00	683.19	673.51
60000	1411.70	949.72	819.30	768.00	745.30	734.73
65000	1529.34	1028.86	887.58	832.00	807.41	795.96
70000	1646.98	1108.01	955.85	896.00	869.51	857.19
75000	1764.62	1187.15	1024.13	960.00	931.62	918.42
80000	1882.26	1266.29	1092.40	1024.00	993.73	979.64
85000	1999.90	1345.44	1160.68	1088.00	1055.84	1040.87
90000	2117.55	1424.58	1228.95	1152.00	1117.95	1102.10
95000	2235.19	1503.72	1297.23	1216.00	1180.05	1163.33
100000	2352.83	1582.87	1365.50	1280.00	1242.16	1224.56
105000	2470.47	1662.01	1433.78	1344.00	1304.27	1285.78
110000	2588.11	1741.15	1502.05	1408.00	1366.38	1347.01
115000	2705.75	1820.30	1570.33	1472.00	1428.49	1408.24
120000	2823.39	1899.44	1638.60	1536.00	1490.60	1469.47
125000	2941.04	1978.58	1706.88	1600.00	1552.70	1530.69
130000	3058.68	2057.73	1775.15	1664.00	1614.81	1591.92
135000	3176.32	2136.87	1843.43	1728.00	1676.92	1653.15
140000	3293.96	2216.02	1911.70	1792.00	1739.03	1714.38
145000	3411.60	2295.16	1979.98	1856.00	1801.14	1775.61
150000	3529.24	2374.30	2048.25	1920.00	1863.24	1836.83
155000	3646.88	2453.45	2116.53	1984.00	1925.35	1898.06
160000	3764.52	2532.59	2184.80	2048.00	1987.46	1959.29
165000	3882.17	2611.73	2253.08	2112.00	2049.57	2020.52
170000	3999.81	2690.88	2321.35	2176.00	2111.68	2081.75
175000	4117.45	2770.02	2389.63	2240.00	2173.79	2142.97
180000	4235.09	2849.16	2457.90	2304.00	2235.89	2204.20
185000	4352.73	2928.31	2526.18	2368.00	2298.00	2265.43
190000	4470.37	3007.45	2594.45	2432.00	2360.11	2326.66
195000	4588.01	3086.59	2662.73	2496.00	2422.22	2387.88
200000	4705.66	3165.74	2731.00	2560.00	2484.33	2449.11
205000	4823.30	3244.88	2799.28	2624.00	2546.43	2510.34
210000	4940.94	3324.02	2867.55	2688.00	2608.54	2571.57
215000	5058.58	3403.17	2935.83	2752.00	2670.65	2632.80
220000	5176.22	3482.31	3004.10	2816.00	2732.76	2694.02
225000	5293.86	3561.45	3072.38	2879.99	2794.87	2755.25
230000	5411.50	3640.60	3140.65	2943.99	2856.97	2816.48
235000	5529.15	3719.74	3208.93	3007.99	2919.08	2877.71
240000	5646.79	3798.88	3277.20	3071.99	2981.19	2938.93
245000	5764.43	3878.03	3345.48	3135.99	3043.30	3000.16
250000	5882.07	3957.17	3413.75	3199.99	3105.41	3061.39

Buying a Home When You're Single

Monthly Payments for
Interest: 15 %
Principal

Principal	5	10	15	20	25	30
1000	23.79	16.13	14.00	13.17	12.81	12.64
5000	118.95	80.67	69.98	65.84	64.04	63.22
10000	237.90	161.33	139.96	131.68	128.08	126.44
15000	356.85	242.00	209.94	197.52	192.12	189.67
20000	475.80	322.67	279.92	263.36	256.17	252.89
25000	594.75	403.34	349.90	329.20	320.21	316.11
30000	713.70	484.00	419.88	395.04	384.25	379.33
35000	832.65	564.67	489.86	460.88	448.29	442.56
40000	951.60	645.34	559.83	526.72	512.33	505.78
45000	1070.55	726.01	629.81	592.56	576.37	569.00
50000	1189.50	806.67	699.79	658.39	640.42	632.22
55000	1308.45	887.34	769.77	724.23	704.46	695.44
60000	1427.40	968.01	839.75	790.07	768.50	758.67
65000	1546.35	1048.68	909.73	855.91	832.54	821.89
70000	1665.30	1129.34	979.71	921.75	896.58	885.11
75000	1784.24	1210.01	1049.69	987.59	960.62	948.33
80000	1903.19	1290.68	1119.67	1053.43	1024.66	1011.56
85000	2022.14	1371.35	1189.65	1119.27	1088.71	1074.78
90000	2141.09	1452.01	1259.63	1185.11	1152.75	1138.00
95000	2260.04	1532.68	1329.61	1250.95	1216.79	1201.22
100000	2378.99	1613.35	1399.59	1316.79	1280.83	1264.44
105000	2497.94	1694.02	1469.57	1382.63	1344.87	1327.67
110000	2616.89	1774.68	1539.55	1448.47	1408.91	1390.89
115000	2735.84	1855.35	1609.53	1514.31	1472.96	1454.11
120000	2854.79	1936.02	1679.50	1580.15	1537.00	1517.33
125000	2973.74	2016.69	1749.48	1645.99	1601.04	1580.56
130000	3092.69	2097.35	1819.46	1711.83	1665.08	1643.78
135000	3211.64	2178.02	1889.44	1777.67	1729.12	1707.00
140000	3330.59	2258.69	1959.42	1843.51	1793.16	1770.22
145000	3449.54	2339.36	2029.40	1909.34	1857.20	1833.44
150000	3568.49	2420.02	2099.38	1975.18	1921.25	1896.67
155000	3687.44	2500.69	2169.36	2041.02	1985.29	1959.89
160000	3806.39	2581.36	2239.34	2106.86	2049.33	2023.11
165000	3925.34	2662.03	2309.32	2172.70	2113.37	2086.33
170000	4044.29	2742.69	2379.30	2238.54	2177.41	2149.55
175000	4163.24	2823.36	2449.28	2304.38	2241.45	2212.78
180000	4282.19	2904.03	2519.26	2370.22	2305.50	2276.00
185000	4401.14	2984.70	2589.24	2436.06	2369.54	2339.22
190000	4520.09	3065.36	2659.22	2501.90	2433.58	2402.44
195000	4639.04	3146.03	2729.19	2567.74	2497.62	2465.67
200000	4757.99	3226.70	2799.17	2633.58	2561.66	2528.89
205000	4876.94	3307.37	2869.15	2699.42	2625.70	2592.11
210000	4995.89	3388.03	2939.13	2765.26	2689.74	2655.33
215000	5114.83	3468.70	3009.11	2831.10	2753.79	2718.55
220000	5233.78	3549.37	3079.09	2896.94	2817.83	2781.78
225000	5352.73	3630.04	3149.07	2962.78	2881.87	2845.00
230000	5471.68	3710.70	3219.05	3028.62	2945.91	2908.22
235000	5590.63	3791.37	3289.03	3094.46	3009.95	2971.44
240000	5709.58	3872.04	3359.01	3160.29	3073.99	3034.67
245000	5828.53	3952.71	3428.99	3226.13	3138.03	3097.89
250000	5947.48	4033.37	3498.97	3291.97	3202.08	3161.11

Term (Years)

Monthly Payments for
Interest: 15.5 %

Principal	5	10	Term (Years) 15	20	25	30
1000	24.05	16.44	14.34	13.54	13.20	13.05
5000	120.27	82.21	71.70	67.69	65.99	65.23
10000	240.53	164.41	143.40	135.39	131.97	130.45
15000	360.80	246.62	215.10	203.08	197.96	195.68
20000	481.06	328.82	286.80	270.78	263.95	260.90
25000	601.33	411.03	358.50	338.47	329.94	326.13
30000	721.60	493.23	430.20	406.16	395.92	391.36
35000	841.86	575.44	501.90	473.86	461.91	456.58
40000	962.13	657.64	573.60	541.55	527.90	521.81
45000	1082.39	739.85	645.30	609.25	593.89	587.03
50000	1202.66	822.05	717.00	676.94	659.87	652.26
55000	1322.93	904.26	788.69	744.63	725.86	717.48
60000	1443.19	986.46	860.39	812.33	791.85	782.71
65000	1563.46	1068.67	932.09	880.02	857.83	847.94
70000	1683.72	1150.87	1003.79	947.72	923.82	913.16
75000	1803.99	1233.08	1075.49	1015.41	989.81	978.39
80000	1924.26	1315.28	1147.19	1083.10	1055.80	1043.61
85000	2044.52	1397.49	1218.89	1150.80	1121.78	1108.84
90000	2164.79	1479.69	1290.59	1218.49	1187.77	1174.07
95000	2285.05	1561.90	1362.29	1286.19	1253.76	1239.29
100000	2405.32	1644.11	1433.99	1353.88	1319.75	1304.52
105000	2525.59	1726.31	1505.69	1421.57	1385.73	1369.74
110000	2645.85	1808.52	1577.39	1489.27	1451.72	1434.97
115000	2766.12	1890.72	1649.09	1556.96	1517.71	1500.19
120000	2886.38	1972.93	1720.79	1624.66	1583.69	1565.42
125000	3006.65	2055.13	1792.49	1692.35	1649.68	1630.65
130000	3126.91	2137.34	1864.19	1760.04	1715.67	1695.87
135000	3247.18	2219.54	1935.89	1827.74	1781.66	1761.10
140000	3367.45	2301.75	2007.59	1895.43	1847.64	1826.32
145000	3487.71	2383.95	2079.29	1963.13	1913.63	1891.55
150000	3607.98	2466.16	2150.99	2030.82	1979.62	1956.78
155000	3728.24	2548.36	2222.69	2098.52	2045.61	2022.00
160000	3848.51	2630.57	2294.38	2166.21	2111.59	2087.23
165000	3968.78	2712.77	2366.08	2233.90	2177.58	2152.45
170000	4089.04	2794.98	2437.78	2301.60	2243.57	2217.68
175000	4209.31	2877.18	2509.48	2369.29	2309.55	2282.90
180000	4329.57	2959.39	2581.18	2436.99	2375.54	2348.13
185000	4449.84	3041.59	2652.88	2504.68	2441.53	2413.36
190000	4570.11	3123.80	2724.58	2572.37	2507.52	2478.58
195000	4690.37	3206.01	2796.28	2640.07	2573.50	2543.81
200000	4810.64	3288.21	2867.98	2707.76	2639.49	2609.03
205000	4930.90	3370.42	2939.68	2775.46	2705.48	2674.26
210000	5051.17	3452.62	3011.38	2843.15	2771.46	2739.49
215000	5171.44	3534.83	3083.08	2910.84	2837.45	2804.71
220000	5291.70	3617.03	3154.78	2978.54	2903.44	2869.94
225000	5411.97	3699.24	3226.48	3046.23	2969.43	2935.16
230000	5532.23	3781.44	3298.18	3113.93	3035.41	3000.39
235000	5652.50	3863.65	3369.88	3181.62	3101.40	3065.61
240000	5772.77	3945.85	3441.58	3249.31	3167.39	3130.84
245000	5893.03	4028.06	3513.28	3317.01	3233.38	3196.07
250000	6013.30	4110.26	3584.98	3384.70	3299.36	3261.29

Index